THE ASTROLOGY BOOK FOR MEN

A GUIDE TO UNDERSTANDING ZODIAC SIGNS, BIRTH CHARTS, HOROSCOPES, AND EVERYTHING ELSE WOMEN ARE TALKING ABOUT

DYLAN WINTON

HENTOPAN
PUBLISHING

© **Copyright 2022 Dylan Winton - All rights reserved.**

The content contained within this book may not be reproduced, duplicated, or transmitted without direct written permission from the author or the publisher.

Under no circumstances will any blame or legal responsibility be held against the publisher, or author, for any damages, reparation, or monetary loss due to the information contained within this book. Either directly or indirectly.

Legal Notice

This book is copyright protected. This book is only for personal use. You cannot amend, distribute, sell, use, quote or paraphrase any part, or the content within this book, without the consent of the author or publisher.

Disclaimer Notice

Please note the information contained within this document is for educational and entertainment purposes only. All effort has been executed to present accurate, up to date, and reliable, complete information. No warranties of any kind are declared or implied. Readers acknowledge that the author is not engaging in the rendering of legal, financial, medical or professional advice. The content within this book has been derived from various sources. Please consult a licensed professional before attempting any techniques outlined in this book.

By reading this document, the reader agrees that under no circumstances is the author responsible for any losses, direct or indirect, which are incurred as a result of the use of the information contained within this document, including, but not limited to, — errors, omissions, or inaccuracies.

CONTENTS

Introduction   7

1. SIGNS AND WONDERS   13
   The History of Astrology   15

2. MEET THE ZODIAC   29
   Aries – The Ram   30
   Taurus – The Bull   31
   Gemini – The Twins   32
   Cancer – The Crab   34
   Leo – The Lion   35
   Virgo – The Virgin   36
   Libra – The Scales   38
   Scorpio – The Scorpion   40
   Sagittarius – The Archer   41
   Capricorn – The Goat   43
   Aquarius – The Water Bearer   44
   Pisces – The Fish   45

3. SPEAKING ASTROLOGICALLY   49
   Your Natal Chart   50
   The Sun   54
   The Moon   55
   Ascendant   59
   The Planets   60
   Retrogrades   68
   The 12 Houses   74

4. THE SUN SIGNS   85
   Aries   86
   Taurus   88
   Gemini   90

Cancer	92
Leo	93
Virgo	95
Libra	96
Scorpio	98
Sagittarius	100
Capricorn	101
Aquarius	103
Pisces	104

5. ASTROLOGY AND RELATIONSHIPS	107
Sun in Aries or Sun in the 1st House	111
Sun in Taurus or Sun in the 2nd House	112
Sun in Gemini or Sun in the 3rd House	113
Sun in Cancer or Sun in the 4th House	115
Sun in Leo or Sun in the 5th House	116
Sun in Virgo or Sun in the 6th House	117
Sun in Libra or Sun in the 7th House	118
Sun in Scorpio or Sun in the 8th House	119
Sun in Sagittarius or Sun in the 9th House	121
Sun in Capricorn or Sun in the 10th House	122
Sun in Aquarius or Sun in the 11th House	123
Sun in Pisces or Sun in the 12th House	124

6. ASTROLOGY AND SUCCESS	127
Moon Phases	127
The Midheaven	130
The Planets	131
Astrology and Careers	137

Final Words	147

SPECIAL OFFER FROM HENTOPAN PUBLISHING

Get this additional book free just for joining the Hentopan Launch Squad.

Hundreds of others are already enjoying early access to all of our current and future books, 100% free.

If you want insider access, plus this free book, all you have to do is Scan the QR code below!

INTRODUCTION

If you're a man reading this book, there's a good chance it was either given to you by a woman, or a woman told you about it. Twice as many women as men follow astrology, and it seems, to me at least, that there's a large percentage of men who just look down their noses at it. Those men think astrology is irrational or just important. Which is ironic, because astrology was developed by men, over thousands of years, who believed what they were doing was highly logical and incredibly important. It was their need to understand the movements of the planets that gave birth to math and science, and it can't get much more logical or important than that.

But when men think about astrology, they often only know about daily horoscopes, which are so broadly written as to be applicable to anyone. Seeing something like, "Someone you know may be going through a difficult time right now. This may pass in a few days", many men discount horoscopes as rubbish.

And you know what? They have a point. Daily horoscopes are written in so that they can appeal to as many people as possible, but that makes them almost useless when anyone tries to apply it to their own personal situation.

That's pretty much the point of view I had about astrology until I started having relationship problems with my then-girlfriend, Rebecca, seven years ago. Our relationship had been great for the previous two years, but lately it seemed like we just weren't on the same page. Little things had started to drive us each crazy. Rebecca was into astrology and kept trying to explain things like, "Mercury is in retrograde", which just went in one ear and out the other. We very nearly ended things, but she convinced me to go to a relationship therapist with her.

I was very hesitant to go, thinking the therapist was going to try and get us to talk about our childhoods or something, or that I would get blamed for our communication problems since I wasn't "open" enough. But that's not how it went. Our therapist was more like a translator, one who luckily spoke astrology. "Mercury in retrograde" was Rebecca's way of explaining that things were difficult right now, but she knew it would pass. If I had known that ahead of time, it would have given me a lot more hope for our future, and maybe a bit more patience, too

In order to better understand my girlfriend, I decided to learn to speak her language. I won't lie, it wasn't easy. Astrology has many, many new terms to learn, like transits, mid-heaven, and ascendants. It also uses terms I thought knew in new ways. Astrology truly is like learning to speak another language. But the further I went, the more fascinated I became. Astrology runs deep! It has many layers, and often factors that subtly influence each other. It couldn't be more different than those daily horoscopes.

I realized that it was about more than just personality typology; it was science and math and psychology all wrapped up into one discipline. And just like math and science, people have been using it for centuries. To me it now has a sort of archaic coolness factor, like Bigfoot or hieroglyphics.

Once I had a better understanding of it, I started using it as a tool, especially during more challenging times of my life. It wasn't long before I started seeing my life and the people in it in a totally new way. Now I'm able to pick up on patterns and articulate those patterns through a unique language. From one guy to another, I want you to know: astrology is cool. It's useful and it's not what you think it is. Many of us used to think of Greek Mythology as cool, right? Well, I promise you'll think the same about astrology after reading this book. In fact, it even has fundamental links to those ancient myths. If you've ever identified with a mythical hero or even one of the characters in *Lord of the Rings*, I can almost guarantee that you will see the value in astrology. The zodiac reveals our personal heroic missions in life. But you wouldn't know this from listening to girls at the mall talk about Sun signs, so I wrote this book to share with other men what it is that is so enticing about astrology.

Astrology has helped me in multiple ways – primarily in communicating with other people, and understanding that some peole just think differently than me. I've actually become so passionate about it that I now do astrology readings. I love musing over the signs and the planets with my clients, but it's disappointing that I can't share my passion with my male friends. In my experience, the astrology community tends to be female-dominated, but trust me, there's value for everyone across all genders. I knew that if men could see astrology through another man's eyes, they'd be able to open their minds and see how truly insightful it is. Take it from me, this is the real deal.

And Rebecca? She's not my girlfriend anymore. She's my wife. What can I say? Our stars were aligned. This book is dedicated to her, but it's written to my past self, and all the men out there like I used to be.

1

SIGNS AND WONDERS

I know what it's like to feel skeptical of astrology. I've been there. Like many proponents, however, I've become so immersed in the language that I can no longer deny its immense value. Ironically, my current relationship with astrology also allows me to see how easy it is for people to dismiss what they don't understand. The zodiac isn't a fad or a simple typology system, though it often appears as such in mainstream culture. I've discovered it's easy to reject the sweeping generalizations of sun-sign horoscopes because they simplify a system that can't be simplified. Astrology is a complicated and incredibly complex system that is best appreciated by digging deep beneath the superficial package it often arrives in. But for people to appreciate it, they must be given the opportunity to participate in it on a greater scale.

People are quick to assume that astrologers believe in an unexplainable magical force, that the planets are emitting a kind of shock wave that controls our choices and our dispositions. Astrologers don't believe in any such thing, but the fact that NASA often feels threatened by these ideas adds fuel to the fire. Astrologers don't believe the planets control us. That's nothing more than a rumor that's been spread by skeptics and the mainstream. There are geographical and astronomical facts, however, that support the real reason why astrology works, even if we can't understand them. The first fact involves the Moon and the tides. We all know that the Moon is responsible for the movement of the tides on Earth's oceans. As humans, we're made up of mostly water. While the Moon isn't zapping us with an invisible laser beam, making us sad during Cancer season and happy when Sagittarius rolls around, it is affecting us in a profound way. Why wouldn't it? After all, life is one giant, complex, water-based organism.

It's also worth mentioning that humans are deeply affected by the Sun's presence in the sky, not just physically, but psychologically. Some people even get Seasonal Affective Disorder (SAD) when there is less sunlight than during the rest of the year. The same principle can be applied to the human psyche. Just like our bodies can't physically survive without sunlight, when we don't allow ourselves to shine, our psyches become lifeless and start to die. In fact, in a recent study published in the *Proceedings of the National Academy of Sciences,* it was reported that the orbits of Venus and Jupiter also have a measurable effect on the climate of Earth. In this study, it states that, "every 405,000 years, due to wobbles in our orbit caused by the gravitational pulls of the two planets, seasonal differences here on Earth become more intense. Summers are hotter and winters colder; dry times drier, wet times wetter." If your Gemini or Virgo friend is looking for facts about why astrology works, keep that anecdote in your pocket.

THE HISTORY OF ASTROLOGY

Astrology has survived millennia - not because of silly horoscopes in women's magazines - but because of its uncanny accuracy and usefulness. Astrology has existed longer than electricity, literature, and modern civilization combined. Before we had calendars or clocks, humans relied on the planets and stars to measure time, seasons, and patterns. It's still used the same way today, only now we have computers to generate natal charts, so we don't have to use as much math or astronomy. At the end of the day, astrology is a lens. It's a way of interpreting the patterns of life through symbolism and meaning. It reveals how connected all life is. Just like we can predict the weather based on an understanding of the earth's atmosphere, we can predict our own human potential and development based on centuries of recorded patterns. We, too, can be tracked like the seasons.

The ancient Babylonians were the first to use astrology, and they did so at a time when it was more normalized than modern politics. But it was also common among ancient Hindu, Chinese, Greek and Roman populations. Ancient people followed the Sun very closely, taking note of its rising and falling every day. They did the same with the Moon, paying careful attention to its various phases to try to get a sense of Earth's timing. This helped them to eventually gain a deeper understanding of the seasons, so they knew when to harvest the appropriate crops. Then, starting in Babylon, astronomers began studying the planets and their movements. In the majority of ancient civilizations, people began noticing patterns. Ultimately, they could infer things about the future based on the patterns they found in the sky.

These people eventually developed a tool called the armillary sphere, a teaching instrument that originated in Greece. Initially, there was a sphere in the center of the device that represented the Earth. But as the models changed and evolved, the inner-sphere came to represent the Sun. Armillary spheres were set to the appropriate latitude by setting the outer meridian rings in a position perpendicular to the horizon and parallel to a line drawn from north to south. Their orientation was established by sighting a celestial object (star, sun, moon or planet) whose position on the ecliptic was known, using a divided ecliptic ring and another ring corresponding to the latitude. The position of a body on the ecliptic could be found using a divided inner latitude ring that held another inner ring that could be turned without disrupting the latitude ring. Needless to say, ancient people put a lot of effort into trying to understand the stars and their effect on humanity. And this wasn't exclusive to Babylonia, either.

The Chinese have long held the values and beliefs of Confucianism, which focuses on the importance of personal ethics and morality. Confucianism laid the foundation for most of Chinese culture, even as it stands today. And its value on the human individual makes it not so different from astrology. Now, the Chinese have their own system with animals symbolically representing each of the calendar years. But the way the Chinese people experience this system is very similar to astrology. For example, the following is taken from "The Origin of the Chinese Zodiac" by journalist Lisa Chiu.

She states:

> "It's been written by Paul Yip, Joseph Lee, and Y.B. Cheung that births in Hong Kong regularly increased, bucking declining trends, to coincide with the birth of a child in a dragon year. Temporary fertility rate increases were seen in the dragon years of 1988 and 2000, they wrote. This is a relatively modern phenomenon as the same increase wasn't seen in 1976, another dragon year."
>
> — LISA CHIU

In the Hindu religion, and in most of India, for that matter, the collective practices Vedic astrology. If you have any experience with astrology, you've probably heard of Vedic astrology. There are even shows on Netflix, such as *Indian Matchmaker*, that capitalize on Vedic astrology. So why is it so popular in India? Well, according to Hindu teachings, all of life is a spiritual journey. Nothing else matters as much as your spiritual development. They also place a great deal of importance on the concept of karma, which is a common term in Western astrology as well. In fact, the Vedas say that a person's karma has a direct link to the position of the planets and stars. Therefore, astrology is a tool to understand the karma that someone came into this life with, and how they're meant to build better karma in their current life to prepare for the next one. Those Hindus who practice it have coined astrology as "the science of fate." That's right. They're even ballsy enough, or perhaps enlightened enough, to call astrology a science!

In ancient Greek and Roman cultures, astrology played a major role as well. It was actually attached to the three major philosophical schools led by Plato, Aristotle, and the Stoics. Each of the lessons provided in the schools grew from the idea that the cosmos is a single, living synthesized organism. The Egyptians also had their own form of astrology, built on the belief that souls would eventually ascend to meet the stars. In some versions of this ancient astrology, the planets were neither influences nor causes of events on Earth, but rather tools to understand and analyze timing. Many famous astrologers still interpret astrology this way today, in other words, as a lens.

According to the Oxford Research Encyclopedias, "astrology had a radical view of time in which the future already existed, at least in potential, and the astrologer's task was to intercede in time, altering the future to human advantage. In this sense, astrology was a form of "participation mystique" in which time and space were conceived of as a single entity and individual and social benefits were to be derived from engaging with it."

It's a lot of work to track the movement of the stars, which just goes to show that people were obsessed with astrology back then. Throughout millennia, people have continued to find value in this tracking system. Even in recent history, men like Ptolemy and JP Morgan have used the stars to time important decisions and seek advice. In fact, JP Morgan once said, "Millionaires don't use astrology. Billionaires do."

Ronald Regan had an in-house astrologer who he would consult for any important business advice. And it's said that Theodore Roosevelt hung his horoscope in the Oval Office. Even Benjamin Franklin found himself fascinated by eclipses and other planetary events. If it's good enough for these brilliant minds, it should be good enough for all of us.

Ptolemy, for example, an ancient Greek mathematician, is an important figure in the history of astrology. He's known as one of the first people to write a comprehensive book on the subject, and he did so while practicing many different disciplines. He was a mathematician, a geographer and astronomer, as well as an astrologer. He was held in extremely high regard in his day, so when he published a book on astrology, that gave it credibility. He was somehow able to present it as both a science and an art--something that would never fly today. Much of Ptolemy's findings were based on astronomy, and more specifically, the unique temperaments of the planets. He observed how the different characteristics of each of the planets had a unique effect on Earth that could be interpreted both symbolically and logically. For example, he noted that Saturn was cold and dry, and also that it has a ring around it. Therefore, it's energy is restricted in both the physical sense and the metaphorical sense.

Ptolemy claimed that since Earth is the source of moisture in the solar system, it's particularly sensitive to the qualities and temperatures of the other planets. He also hypothesized that the consistent and cyclical movement of the planets formed an unpredictable atmosphere that no doubt had an effect on all of life on Earth. The way he explained it is similar to how most astrologers explain it: "Just as two similar seeds grow differently as a result of their environment, so is each soul affected by the celestial atmosphere at the time of its birth. In the principle of sympathy and antipathy, the aspects and movement of the stars continue to produce favorable or injurious conditions determined by the individual's personal disposition."

Another prominent figure in our history made great strides in giving astrology the credibility it deserves-- Carl Jung. Jung was deeply inspired by astrology and considered it often when forming his psychological findings. In fact, many astrologers practice Jungian astrology today--a form that combines Jung's psychological findings with astrology.

There are even published letters between Sigmund Freud and Carl Jung (who were friends when they were both alive) that articulate the significance of astrology in Carl Jung's findings. Jung was always quite mystical, and he believed that there was a strong nature component to the human psyche, whereas Freud placed greater value on the concept of "nurture."

Jung shared the following in a letter to Freud:

"I dare say that we shall one day discover in astrology a good deal of knowledge that has been intuitively projected into the heavens.

For instance, it appears that the signs of the zodiac are character pictures, in other words, libido symbols which depict the typical qualities of the libido at a given moment..."

— CARL JUNG ; JUNE 12, 1911

And he later stated:

"Astrology is of particular interest to the psychologist since it contains a sort of psychological experience which we call projected – this means that we find the psychological facts as it were in the constellations. This originally gave rise to the idea that these factors derive from the stars, whereas they are merely in a relation of synchronicity with them. I admit that this is a very curious fact which throws a peculiar light on the structure of the human mind."

— CARL G. JUNG IN 1947 IN A LETTER TO PROF. B.V. RAMAN

It's easy to be skeptical of astrology. In my opinion, it's harder to open your mind, which is why so many people are resistant. It's a shame, though, because it's a tool unlike anything else. The Myers-Briggs personality test, for example, doesn't have the same kind of rich history that is based on the timing of life around us. Neither does any typology system, for that matter. Astrology can be used in a number of different ways, and it can help us understand the people in our life. My suggestion is to set aside your skepticism and give it a chance, like so many great minds in history have. Let's face it, for something to maintain such relevance for centuries, it must have some profound value.

Following are quotes by intelligent, successful men. Hopefully, you find them inspiring, and perhaps even amusing:

> *"About astrology and palmistry: they are good because they make people vivid and full of possibilities. They are communism at its best. Everybody has a birthday and almost everybody has a palm."*
>
> — KURT VONNEGUT

"Astrology had an important role in the ancient world. You can't understand many things unless you know something about astrology—the plays of Shakespeare and so on."

— STEVEN PINKER, CANADIAN PSYCHOLOGIST

"We are merely the stars' tennis-balls, struck and banded which way please them."

— JOHN WEBSTER

"We need not feel ashamed of flirting with the zodiac. The zodiac is well worth flirting with."

— D.H. LAWRENCE

"Without astrology, man treads, as it were, in the dim twilight of ignorance."

— LUKE DENNIS BROUGHTON, ENGLISH ASTROLOGER

"Yes, astrology is easy, laughably easy, to debunk using conventional methods and ideas. On the other hand, and this is really the subtext of the entire social science debate...convention is a poor guide to anything."

— MARTIN COHEN, BRITISH PHILOSOPHER

"I admit it: as a sane and rational human being, I continue to be baffled as to why astrology works... But I wouldn't be doing this for a living if astrology didn't keep working, consistently, over and over again. Frankly, I'd much rather be a plumber. Being a plumber pays well and only involves getting up to *your ankles in sewage, not in people's love lives. Believe me, sewage is a lot easier to deal with."*

— MATTHEW CURRIE, ASTROLOGER,
COUNSELOR, AND WRITER

2

MEET THE ZODIAC

As the Earth travels around the Sun each year, the Sun appears to pass in front of 12 constellations. This collection of constellations is referred to as the Zodiac, and figuring out which is your Sun sign is usually where people start when they begin learning about astrology. You'll find out more about the sun signs in Chapter 4, but in this chapter we'll take a look at the mythology behind each zodiac symbol. Learning the myths behind the signs can help you better understand why they're associated with certain personality traits.

Each of the constellations is also linked to one of the four elements from classical philosophy – Air, Fire, Water, and Earth. The elements are the "broad strokes" of astrology, which means that if you know the element linked to a constellation, you know the most basic aspect of that sign. Fire signs are dynamic and passionate, earth signs are physical and sensual, air signs are cerebral and communicative, and water signs are emotional and loving. However, there's a big difference between constellations that share the same element, as we're about to see.

ARIES – THE RAM

Each of the twelve zodiac signs reflects the times and seasons under which they were born. For example, Aries is the first sign of the zodiac, because it marks the very first day of spring, kicking life into action both physically and symbolically. In other words, the blossoming of life in springtime reflects the same qualities for which the Aries personality is known. Aries is also one of three fire signs. Personality-wise, Aries are quick, reactive, excitable, and all about action. Its symbol, taken from its constellation, is the ram, which further illustrates the driven nature of this archetype. Every zodiac sign can also be linked to mythology, revealing profound insights about the temperament's strengths and weaknesses.

Aries is commonly associated with Greek mythology and the flying ram that rescued twins Phrixus and Helle from their wicked stepmother. The ram carried them on its back toward Colchis but Helle fell off and drowned in the sea. Phrixus made it to his destination safely, then sacrificed the ram and hung its fleece in a sacred grove protected by a dragon. This is the fleece of the Jason and the Golden Fleece myth. Jason and his Argonauts had to face many battles in their quest for this sacred relic, which is a symbol of authority and kingship. It is this quest that captures the spirit of Aries. Astrologer Liz Greene states, "This golden fleece, and Jason's quest for it, seem to portray the theme of the slaying of the Old Father, and the quest for individual spiritual identity, which I feel to be at the core of the drama of Aries the Ram.".

TAURUS – THE BULL

After fiery Aries comes earthy Taurus. Taurus people are often passionate like Aries. The big difference, though, is that Taurus is passionate with strong opinions. Tauruses tend to be obsessed with politics and their beliefs. Taurus is notoriously stubborn, and throughout life it tends to remain set in its ways. Think of the tortoise in the "Tortoise and the Hare" fable. The tortoise didn't win the race by adapting well or being the quickest. Just like the tortoise, Taurus succeeds through steadfast determination and follow-through. Taurus is also the sign of values. If Aries is about raw power and spiritual identity, Taurus is about expanding that identity through a strong sense of likes and dislikes. Did I mention Taurus is opinionated?

Taurus's symbol is the bull because of a Greek myth that revolves around the Cretan Bull. Minos, son of Zeus, in order to confirm his right over his brothers to rule Crete, prayed to Poseidon to send a sign. Poseidon sent a magical bull, but instructed Minos to sacrifice the bull as a sacred offering. When the bull arrived, though, Minos felt the bull was too fine a specimen to be sacrificed and kept it for himself, instead offering a normal bull to Poseidon. Again, whenever we're dealing with Taurus, we're dealing with an 'I want it, gotta have it' personality type. Of course, Poseidon noticed and retaliated by casting a spell that made Minos' wife, Pasiphae, fall in love with the bull. The bull and Minos' wife gave birth to the half-bull, half-human we know of today as a Minotaur, which then laid waste to the land. Through his stubbornness and greed, King Minos had created a world of chaos. This is Taurus's fatal flaw. Taurus has the best taste of all the zodiac signs, but it can get carried away by its obsessive desires.

GEMINI – THE TWINS

Gemini is the third sign of the zodiac, and it gets a lot of heat for being flighty and two-faced. That's because

Gemini is more interested in learning new things than in creating a strict identity for itself. It's a mutable sign, which means that, like Virgo, Sagittarius and Pisces, it needs freedom and the ability to redefine itself over and over again. Geminis tend to be impatient, easily bored, and thirsty for new information or gossip. They are like children who can't stop asking their parents questions. They have endless curiosity and a biting sense of humor. Most are quick-witted and tend toward sarcasm. They're experts at language and know how to use their words to get their point across. Symbolically, Gemini is known as the astrological twins. It understands that humans are complicated, and can be one way one day, and the opposite the next.

The myth associated with Gemini follows twins, Castor and Pollux. Though they had the same mother, Pollux was the son of Zeus, and was therefore a demigod, while Castor was the son of Tyndareus, King of Sparta. When Castor was killed in battle, Pollux pleaded with Zeus to bring him back. Zeus agrees to immortalize them both, as long as they spend half their time on Earth and the other half among the stars in the heavens. This is why part of Gemini's life theme involves opposites.

CANCER – THE CRAB

Cancer is the fourth sign of the zodiac and the first water sign, so it tends to be more emotional than its predecessors. Cancer is also ruled by the Moon, so Cancer individuals need a lot of comfort and safety. These are the people who tend to spend a lot of time in the garden, nurturing the life around them. Or they might be obsessed with their pets. They love a solid home base and find it easy to be nurturing. They also have a dark sense of humor. Many famous comedians are Cancers or Scorpios, with an impressive ability to turn their heavy emotions into self-deprecating jokes. They're good at being emotionally supportive, whether through humor or direct comfort. But first and foremost, they need to emotionally support themselves.

Cancers aren't as confrontational as, say, Scorpios. Cancer's symbol is the crab, so it tends to approach issues sideways, pinching them with its claws before quickly exiting the scene. In the mythological tale of the Twelve Labors of Hercules, Hercules is battling a nine-headed serpentine monster named Hydra, when Hera, wife of Zeus, sends a crab to harass him. The crab sneak attacks Hercules' feet and ankles, allowing Hydra to make progress until Hercules stomps on it. Hera rewards the crab for its bravery by placing it in the heavens as a constellation. The myth illustrates how

Cancers handle confrontation, which can sometimes be considered passive-aggressive. You'll be aware of their feelings whether or not they explicitly express them. But beyond that, Cancer loves closeness and connection. After all, its symbol resembles a sideways 69. Make of that what you will.

LEO – THE LION

Next in line is Leo. Leo's ruling planet is the Sun, so it's no surprise that these individuals love to shine. Many are natural performers or actors. Most crave passion and excitement, and they know how to party better than any other sign. Leos generally radiate a natural warmth, which again reflects the life-giving power of the Sun. They have a reputation for needing lots of attention. But depending on a Leo's upbringing, they can be either introverted or extroverted. Many Leos are shy, but secretly long to be noticed for their natural talents. More than anything, though, Leos are fun, childlike, and authentic. Their purpose in life is to connect with their unique authenticity and express it as creatively as possible.

Leo is also often associated with the myth of the Twelve Labors of Hercules. All three of the fire signs (Aries, Leo, and Sagittarius) have a heroic quality to them. This is because they inherently long to feel special. They want to use their raw and reactive power in some way. As the myth goes, Hercules is driven mad by Hera and kills his wife and children, but when he recovers from his madness, he asks how he can atone for his actions. He is told he must perform twelve impossible labors given to him by King Eurystheus. Each time he performs a labor, he nearly fails until some creative realization strikes him like a lightning bolt. His first labor is to slay the invincible Namean Lion, which happens to be Leo's astrological symbol. Hercules tries several methods to kill this lion, but ultimately, he strangles it with his bare hands. This is a testament to Leos' courage and tenacity. Of all the signs, Leo is probably the most courageous.

VIRGO – THE VIRGIN

After Leo comes the analytical Virgo. Like Gemini, Virgo is ruled by Mercury, so Virgo has the same mercurial knack for language and systems. Steve Jobs was a Virgo who used his extreme attention to detail to make Apple products the sleekest, most user-friendly technology on the market. Virgos are known for being helpful, but they're also experts at organizing people and things. They can look at a system and understand all the parts that make up the whole. Details are their thing. Along the same vein, Virgos also tend toward perfectionism, and have a strong relationship to their bodies and physical health. Next to Scorpio, Virgo is probably the most sexual of all the signs because of the sign's connection to the physical body.

Virgo's symbol is the virgin, which also says something about the archetype's relationship to sex. Keith Raniere, leader of sex-cult NXIVM, is a Virgo who used his understanding of psychology to manipulate a large group of women into performing sexual favors for him. Sometimes, Virgos crave physical satisfaction so much that they'll go to great lengths to achieve it. You're probably wondering; if Virgos love sex so much, why is their symbol the virgin? It may seem like a paradox but that's because we have to reinterpret the concept of the virgin.

Virgos have a virginal quality, not because they're prudish, but because they have a deep appreciation of their own bodies and know that no one can take that away from them. There's an abundance of Virgos in sex work, for example, because Virgos realize they can offer their bodies as a service, receive earthy gratification from that service and continue on with their lives without any guilt. Of course, this is a sweeping generalization, but this attitude does tend to be common among Virgos.

In Greek mythology, Virgo is associated with the maiden goddess Astraea, who was the daughter of Zeus and lived during the Golden Age on Earth, when there was only peace. But as the ordinary human men grew corrupt, Astraea grew frustrated. She tried urging the humans to obey nature's laws but eventually gave up, opting to leave Earth and go to Heaven instead. This story reveals Virgo's critical lens, as well as its relationship to the earthly world. Virgos often feel they know what's best, and more often than not, they tend to be right.

LIBRA – THE SCALES

Libra follows Virgo and carries a very different energy. If Virgo loves sex, Libra loves romance. This is because Libra's symbol is the scale. It's all about one thing compared to another, fair vs. unfair, just vs. unjust. Basically, Libra is the lawyer of the zodiac.

Libras love relationships for this same reason, to balance their own personalities by relating to their other half; to learn more about themselves through the eyes of another. Libra is also Venus-ruled, so it craves harmony and beauty in all things. Plus, it's an Air sign, so it enjoys intellectual conversations. Sometimes Libras can be overly obsessed with their appearance. If you know a lot of gym rats, consider how many of them have birthdays in early October. By the same token, many Libras can rub people the wrong way with their hyper-positivity. These are the women who are so bubbly, you wonder if their face gets sore from all the smiling. If you get to know Libras on a deeper level, though, you'll see that all that positivity has a threshold. Libras are all smiles and sweetness until the scale becomes too lop-sided.

Oddly enough, Libra's constellation used to be recognized as part of Scorpio's claws called Chelae. Libra wasn't established as its own constellation until long after the other zodiac signs. Astrologer Liz Greene says the following about this:

> *"It is very suggestive: that the scales of balanced judgment should have developed from what was originally the gripping organ of the dark underworld creature which has always represented the chthonic realm. It is as though our noble faculty of judgment emerged from something much older, more archaic and more primitive, and evolved over time into what we now understand as objective or impartial assessment."*
>
> — ASTROLOGER LIZ GREENE

The myth associated with Libra follows Homer's hero, a nobleman named Paris. Zeus, unwilling to show favoritism, chose Paris to judge a beauty contest between Hera, Athena, and Aphrodite. Being a fair and balanced Libra, Paris tried to choose fairly but couldn't make up his mind, so instead he chose Aphrodite because she promised him the most beautiful wife of all--Helen of Troy. This enraged Helen's husband (yes, she was already married), and set off the Trojan War. This obviously sheds some light on Libra's indecisiveness, but also on how vital it is for the Libra personality to weigh all options and strive for true balance.

SCORPIO – THE SCORPION

Scorpio is a relationship sign and, like the scorpion that it's symbolically associated with, it packs a sting. Scorpio is the sign of intensity and transformation. They're the people with 'crazy eyes', or heavy energy that alters the dynamic of any room they walk into. Scorpios are deep, but because they're intensely emotional, they're also obsessive. Scorpio often reacts to any possibility of getting hurt by enlisting its scorpion pincers and harnessing some semblance of power over things. Many politicians are Scorpios--they have a knack for holding power and they're also great at keeping secrets. Many Scorpios have some kind of darkness in their background, making them extra sensitive to all that is dark and mysterious. Scorpios are often true crime enthusiasts. If you know someone who is obsessed with serial killers, they're probably a Scorpio!

As far as Scorpio mythology goes, many myths are applicable. Generally, any story that deals with the conquering of a dragon has Scorpio themes. This is because Scorpio must constantly come face to face with darkness, often its own darkness, in order to transform and rise anew from the ashes. Hercules had to battle the Hydra; Siegfried, a legendary Germanic hero, slayed a dragon; and Perseus, son of Zeus, beheaded the monster Medusa. Each of these stories captures the epic battle that Scorpio must often engage in with itself. It is Scorpio's job to accept its darkness and accomplish something powerful through it, like becoming a true crime investigator.

SAGITTARIUS – THE ARCHER

Sagittarius is the ninth sign and it's ruled by the largest planet, Jupiter. This is important because Sagittarius is known for being big in every way. This sign wants to constantly expand, through travel, learning, spending lots of money all at once. If it's bigger and better, Sagittarius wants it. These people have loads of optimism and personality. They're often energetic, bold, and talkative with a dry sense of humor. These are also your stoner, philosopher types. They're on a quest for truth and meaning, whether they're aware of it or not.

Because Sagittarius is always seeking expansion, it runs the risk of overdoing it. Many people born in late November or early-mid December have trouble with extremes. They may spend and spend until they have nothing left, or overestimate their own abilities. Even so, they bounce back quickly and always do so with optimism and generosity. Much like Gemini, Sagittarius is hard to pin down for too long. It's constantly on the move, looking for bigger and better things, or more profound truths. This is why its symbol as the centaur is quite fitting.

Centaurs are half-human, half-horse. Chiron was a centaur born to Kronos, King of the Titans, and was immortal. But then one of Hercules' arrows that had been dipped in hydra venom falls on Chiron's foot and poisons him. Though Chiron was a master of the healing arts, he was unable to heal himself, and relinquished his immortality. Seeing this, Zeus took pity on him and placed him among the stars to be honored. This reveals a similar theme to that of Scorpio. With so much light and optimism, there must also be darkness. But the centaur also carries a bow and arrow, so as long as Sagittarius aims for ultimate truth, it can remain optimistic and focused. Focus is not easy for Sagittarius, but like the centaur, they are capable.

CAPRICORN – THE GOAT

Capricorn is vastly different from Sagittarius. In fact, you can think of Capricorn as the sign that comes along afterward to clean up the mess Sagittarius made while partying too hard. Capricorn prefers rules and order. Although, some Capricorns still have a touch of the rebel deep inside which they might express through things like tattoos, or foul language, or a love of rock music. Stereotypically, though, Capricorns tend to be the goody-two-shoes. They often worry about the future and whether or not they have enough security to survive in this world. But because of this fine attention to rules and order, Capricorns make great leaders. At worst, they're teachers' pets. At best, they're the responsible person in charge, the neighbor who has extra face masks when a pandemic hits. These individuals are hard-working, ambitious and resilient. Like its symbol, the goat, a Capricorn's steadfast approach usually wins out.

Capricorn is identified with the goat-nymph Amalthea, sister of the god Pan, a satyr (half-goat, half-man). As the myth goes, Titan siblings Rhea and Kronos married, but Kronos soon received a prophecy that one of his children would depose him, so he ate each one as soon as they were born. To protect her infant Zeus from Kronos, Rhea hid him on Crete, to be nurtured by Amalthea. At one point, the child Zeus accidentally broke off one of Amalthea's horns, so to make up for this he later endowed this broken horn with the power to be filled with whatever its owner desired. This is what we know of today as the "horn of plenty," or the cornucopia. Amalthea was eventually rewarded for her service to Zeus by being made a constellation.

AQUARIUS – THE WATER BEARER

Aquarius is the eleventh sign of the zodiac. Many great inventors throughout history have been Aquarians because they strive to experience the world in their own original way. They're known for being great collaborators and humanitarians. If your friend group can't stop fighting, bring an Aquarius in to mediate the situation. Aquarius is the last air sign, so it loves to intellectualize and can sometimes does this a bit too much. This is why Aquarians have a reputation for being detached or aloof from their immediate surroundings. They often neglect relationships because they're so busy trying to implement broad change or reform.

It makes sense then that Aquarius is tied to the Greek god, Prometheus. As a god, Prometheus resided in the heavens, but he also spent a great deal of time among the mortals on earth. This speaks to Aquarius's sociability and need for friendship. Aquarius also tends to be nonjudgmental and accepting of all. When Prometheus learned that humans did not have access to fire, he took it upon himself to steal it from the gods and give it to the mortals on earth, who he knew would find it quite valuable. He was severely punished, of course, as Aquarians often are for their rebelliousness. But in the end, he gave something of significance to the larger collective, which is what Aquarius craves more than anything.

PISCES – THE FISH

Pisces is the final sign of the zodiac and can be the most confusing. It's almost like Pisces has a little bit of all the signs rolled into one. It's highly emotional, so can fluctuate and change depending on the mood or the season. Many Pisces are notoriously tardy and are sometimes perceived as liars because they're like the ocean, moving according to the tide.

Pisces can also be needy. As the last sign, they long for something greater, more profound, more emotional. They're romantics, and love to lose themselves in things, whether it's art, drugs, or relationships. Essentially, they want to transcend reality. So if you're wondering why your Pisces friend never responds to your texts, it's because they're busy daydreaming or getting high. Pisces are motivated by being needed. They love to feel emotionally connected to others, which often manifests in them saving or healing others. They make great therapists and teachers.

Pisces' astrological symbol is the fish, which makes sense, given that fish spend their days in the ocean, which is mystical and vast. In the Greek myth, Aphrodite and her son Eros flee from the monster Typhon, who is rampaging around Mount Olympus, by jumping into the Euphrates River. We then have two versions of this tale, one that says they are rescued by fish and the other that says they disguise themselves as fish, but both explain that their tails are tied together so they will not lose each other in the Euphrates. This explains why Pisces tend to hate separation. If they had it their way, no one would ever be alone. Either way, Aphrodite repaid the fish for their kindness by giving them a place in the sky.

Each of the twelve signs of the zodiac has its own quirks, strengths and weaknesses. It's impossible to say that one sign is better than any other because they're all so fundamentally different. But that's why astrology is cool; it celebrates our differences while allowing us to poke fun at one another. Each sign serves an important purpose, and the myths associated with them highlight this. Astrology can help us realize how bad-ass we all are. Just like Zeus or Prometheus, we all have unique personalities with unique skill sets and things to accomplish according to those skill sets. This brings us to the exploration of the natal chart, which is so complex, and yet specific, that it will no doubt help you understand why humans are the messy and complicated creatures that we are.

3

SPEAKING ASTROLOGICALLY

Astrology has a language all its own. If you've overheard your girlfriends discussing people's signs, you may understand what I mean. "He's a Scorpio?!" "Yeah, but he has a Mars/Pluto conjunction in Aquarius." This is just one example of the unique verbiage that sets the amateurs apart from the pros.

The terminology can seem daunting at first, but with a little knowledge of basic math and geometry, you can read a natal chart in no time. You'd be surprised how easy it is to analyze and articulate a natal chart that, on first impression, looks like a weird and complicated graph.

YOUR NATAL CHART

I bet you've been wondering for a while now – just what is a natal chart? A natal chart is the bread and butter of astrology. The twelve sun signs that we've just discussed are merely the tip of the iceberg. The natal chart is the entire map of the iceberg, including all the surrounding areas. If you were to ever purchase an astrology reading, the natal chart would form the basis of the reading.

Essentially, it's a blueprint of the stars' positions at the time and place of your birth. It shows what planets were near which constellations at the moment you were born, and how those planets interact with one another symbolically and psychologically. I'll explore the symbolic significance of each planet later on. For now, let's break down the chart and learn how to interpret it.

A natal chart, otherwise known as a birth chart, is sort of like a wheel, where every sign is accounted for. It looks like this:

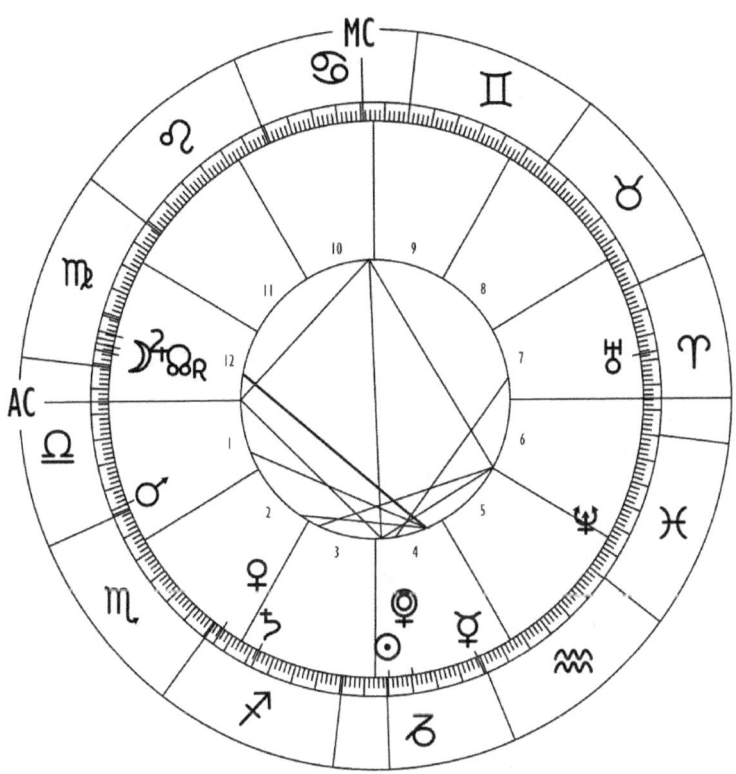

As you can see, each of the twelve signs is shown along the outer edge of the circle, represented by their glyphs (symbols). On this chart, Libra is on the ascendant (AC), which means Libra was the constellation rising above the horizon at the moment of this individual's birth. Libra falls in the 1st house of the birth chart, which you can see from the numbers located on the inner circle. The rest of the signs are then organized in order, going counter-clockwise.

No matter what your rising sign (or ascendant) is, the order of the signs will never change. The position of their houses will simply rotate according to the rising sign. The rising sign is determined by the precise minute you were born, and it is always the starting point of any natal chart.

If you don't know your rising sign, you can't assign planets or signs to any of the houses. This is because the position of the houses and the placement of the signs in your chart depends entirely on which sign is placed in the 1st house. This is always the left-most point on the chart, so where the chart above says AC, which stands for ascendant. Now you know why women who are into astrology ask you if you know what time you were born. The ascendant changes every few hours, so an accurate birth time is key. With the rising sign in place at the nine o'clock position, all of the other signs fall into their designated houses and you can start analyzing where the planets fall.

I should clarify that you can identify most of your planet's sign positions based on your birthday alone. You can simply Google where the planets were on the day you were born. But if you want the full natal chart experience, with the rising sign and houses, you need a precise time of birth. Plus, the moon changes signs every two days, so the moon sign might also be inaccurate without a proper time of birth. And the moon sign is one of the most important factors in astrology, so it's worth it to consult your birth certificate.

In the example image above, you can see that there are tiny symbols positioned in various signs/houses. These symbols reflect each of the nine planets. There are a few other symbols as well, such as the north node and Chiron, but the planets are the most important symbols. The first planet to look out for is the sun. Chances are you already know your sun sign, sometimes referred to as your star sign, but in the context of the natal chart, you can now see which house your sun falls into. In the above example, the sun is in Capricorn in the fourth house. We know this because the sun's glyph is a circle with a dot in the center.

Since the sun is close to the edge of the 3rd house, it can be considered "on the cusp" of the fourth, or in "the first decant" of Capricorn. This means that you can interpret it with a bit more nuance. This individual may feel a strong connection to fourth house activities, such as nurturing their family members, but with a 3rd house slant. So while they love the comfort of family, they may also have the urge to shine using their knowledge and communication.

THE SUN

The Sun shows where we feel most alive. Its placement indicates in which area of life we're meant to shine as individuals. It also shows where we are meant to encounter themes that will facilitate our ego development. In essence, it points to our basic personality temperament. What most people don't realize, however, is that developing the traits of the sun sign is a life-long process. Since it reflects the ego, its energy requires constant growth and attunement. Each sign has the potential for mature and immature expression. Cultivating a mature relationship with your sun sign tends to be a lengthy process. The moon sign, on the other hand, is a different story.

THE MOON

The Moon, unlike the Sun, reflects the subconscious. It points to who you are when no one's looking. According to the above example, the moon is in Virgo in the 12th house. So this individual would feel like a Virgo, despite the Capricorn ego expression. The moon also shows how we process and experience emotions. Someone with a Virgo moon would tend to approach emotions analytically. They would make emotional decisions based on logic. It's placement in the 12th house complicates matters, but we'll discuss that later.

Unlike the sun sign, the moon sign usually requires little conscious development. Typically, we don't have to work to get in touch with the qualities of our moon sign because it reflects the subconscious--our natural feeling process. But if the energies reflected in the rest of your chart contradict the energies reflected by your moon sign, getting in touch with the qualities may prove more challenging. The moon is also associated with the mother archetype. So the sign your moon falls in shows how you can nurture yourself.

Moon Phases

There's much you can learn about your own emotional world based on the moon phase you were born under. It's not common for people to know their moon phase. Many people know their moon signs, especially these days, but the moon phases get less attention in the astrology world. Still, knowing your moon phase can illuminate you as to why you approach emotional concerns the way you do. Following are the moon phases, and what each reveals symbolically about the way you deal with your emotions. You can determine your moon phase by simply Googling to find out what shape the moon took on your birthday.

New Moon

If you were born under a New Moon, the energy associated with "newness" will be at the core of your personality. Your emotional world will be more spontaneous than other people's. And you may have sudden intuitions that tell you exactly what you should do next. You might also have more new beginnings than you do finished projects and an abundance of ideas all the time. Following through, however, can prove difficult for you. These people tend to have an optimism that isn't always present in other moon types. They see life as a series of endless possibilities. They don't feel as restricted as some of the other types, but facing reality can be challenging.

Crescent Moon

Those born under a Crescent Moon have a bit of work to do. Since it follows the new moon phase, these individuals need to work through some of the baggage from the past in order to follow through and be successful. They tend to value security and comfort, which further necessitates the need to process the past. But the crescent moon is also the start of a growth process. If these people can learn how to be independent and trust their gut the way new moon types do, then there's no stopping them from achieving the life of their dreams. Often, they're good at getting past the new stage, meaning they can have a great idea, and even implement it, but as soon as insecurity or setbacks occur, they may feel defeated. Crescent Moons often have to fight against this feeling and learn to trust themselves and their ability to see things through to the end.

First Quarter Moon

According to the website Cafe Astrology, "The First Quarter Moon can be referred to as "crisis in action." Its challenge is to restructure chaos into new forms. These individuals have a knack for overcoming scary situations. When an emergency occurs, they can step up and transform a bad situation into a good one. They're the fighters in the fight or flight scenario. Obviously, these are amazing qualities to have. But it's also important to note that these people thrive on a bit of drama, so much so that they may subconsciously create it. These are the people who become firefighters and paramedics. They have the wisdom and courage from the first two moon phases to assist them through life.

Gibbous Moon

People born under the Gibbous Moon phase are inherent perfectionists. It's not enough for them to understand subjects at a surface level, they want to know exactly how everything works from top to bottom. They find great joy in learning and understanding things, which proves helpful in a wide variety of fields. They make great leaders or entrepreneurs, for example. Sometimes, these people can have anxious energy, especially when they don't know all the facts or details. But once they master a subject or puzzle, they feel on top of the world. They're interested in the truth above all else.

Full Moon

Full Moons are all about completion. People born under a full moon understand the necessity to have something to show for themselves. It's not enough to just have an idea or a strong intuition, full moon people are interested in the end result. Additionally, these individuals tend to be idealists. They can see the final product with more clarity than anyone else, and they want that product to have meaning to them and the rest of the world. The urge to complete things of value runs very deep in these individuals. And they can be disappointed when things turn out less than ideal. This is especially true in romantic relationships. But Full Moon people are determined, and usually successful.

ASCENDANT

The sign that's placed on your ascendant, or the rising sign, is also important. Not just because it decides the format of your whole chart, but because it symbolically shows how you present yourself to the world. The rising sign is like the mask we wear. It's who we are with acquaintances and it's the first impression we give off. It also indicates what we hone in on in life, or how we perceive the world around us. In the example chart, the individual has Libra rising. So the qualities of Libra color this person's worldview. As we learned earlier, they will be very attuned to what's fair and unfair.

Harmony is something they seek, and they'll go out of their way to surround themselves with beauty. The rising sign also indicates your life path, since it suggests how you perceive the world around you. If you perceive life through a Libran lens, you'll want to pursue a life that is based on Libran qualities. Many astrologers also believe that the rising sign is the means toward cultivating the entire personality. In other words, if you struggle to synthesize all the different functions in your chart, you can lean into your rising sign to feel more whole and complete.

THE PLANETS

The sun, moon, and rising sign are what many astrology practitioners refer to as "the big three." They're the fundamental building blocks of the personality. The rest of the planets color the personality as well, though. And depending on their placement in your birth chart, some may affect your temperament more than others. In the example above, the individual has the sun placed near the planet Pluto. Therefore, the characteristics of Pluto will affect them more than someone who has no planets near their sun. Each of the planets represents very specific qualities. Let's discuss each one in-depth.

Mercury

Mercury is the first of what are called the personal planets. These planets, (Mercury, Venus, and Mars) travel close to the sun, so they are felt more personally as a counterpart or facilitator to the ego's development. Mercury rules Gemini and Virgo, so it has a brainy, curious nature. It's the planet of communication, language, and processing information. Its placement in the natal chart shows where we are thirsty to learn new things, and it also reveals our unique style of communication.

For example, if Mercury falls in Pisces, you may interpret information more emotionally than someone with Mercury in Taurus. If Mercury falls in your 10th house, you may feel inclined to make a career out of communication. If it falls in the 5th, you may prefer to communicate through an artistic medium. You'll want to interpret each planet based on the sign *and* the house it falls in to get the most detailed interpretation. You'll learn all about the houses later in this chapter.

Venus

Venus is the next personal planet and one of the more popular planets in astrology. Unlike detached Mercury, Venus is the planet of love. More specifically, though, it's the planet of values. Wherever Venus falls in your natal chart shows what kind of things you're attracted to. It also shows what you find most valuable in life. And since it's Libra's ruling planet, it indicates where we can go to strive for balance. As the planet of love and attraction, it can also show the qualities we look for in a partner.

If Venus falls in Leo in your birth chart, you'll probably be attracted to people with a lot of confidence and pride. If Venus falls in Scorpio, you'll likely value a deep connection with a partner. Additionally, you might be attracted to Scorpio activities, and may find great value in psychoanalyzing the people around you. Aesthetically, you may be inclined toward darker or edgy styles. In short, once you've learned how to fully interpret your chart, you'll be able to understand more about yourself and the choices you make.

Mars

Mars is the final personal planet. Venus is almost like Mars' counterpart. Mars rules Aries, so its placement shows where we need to take action and use our masculine energy in order to get things done. Wherever it falls in your birth chart illuminates how you go about getting the things you want in life.

If Mars falls in Aries for you, you'll attack your goals very directly, with speed and without over-thinking. If it falls in Cancer, however, you may approach things more sensitively. Going after what you want may be more of an emotional process. Mars can also reveal insights about *what* it is you want. If Mars falls in Aquarius, for example, you may use your fiery energy and natural drive to achieve freedom. If it falls in Capricorn, you may have a lot of energy and drive when it comes to career ambitions. Mars shows us where we're willing to fight for our desires. It also shows the style in which we achieve those desires.

Jupiter

♃

Jupiter is the first of two social planets. The social planets are concerned with functioning well within society. Jupiter represents the need to expand within society, while Saturn represents the need to discipline or scale back. Their energies aren't felt as personally as the personal signs, which facilitate ego expression, and this is why you may not feel the qualities of these planet placements as strongly as your Mercury, Venus, or Mars placements. They're less attached to your personality. Even so, these planets can shed a lot of light on how you relate to the world at large.

Jupiter is especially illuminating in terms of our relationship to abundance. Jupiter, which rules Sagittarius, has the urge to constantly expand. So wherever Jupiter falls in your birth chart, that is where you have a constant desire to grow and enlarge your scope of activity. If it falls in Taurus, you'll likely feel the need to constantly build more and more security for yourself. If it falls in Pisces, you may become addicted to your own imagination – constantly dreaming up new plans without ever executing on them. Jupiter also shows where we tend toward extremes, but the flip side of that is boundless optimism.

Saturn

Saturn can be seen as the opposite of Jupiter. Saturn rules Capricorn and it represents restriction, discipline, and limitations. So wherever Saturn falls shows where we have to work extra hard to mature, because Capricorn is all about responsibility and authority. So Saturn points to the areas of life in which we need to take responsibility, but also where we have the capacity to master that realm. For example, if Saturn falls in Virgo in your birth chart, you may feel restricted by details. Or perhaps you find taking care of your physical health to be a limiting and difficult practice.

If Saturn falls in Gemini, you may have difficulty with communication, or you may find school especially difficult. Ultimately, though, this planet challenges us to work hard, take responsibility, and overcome our limitations. Additionally, wherever Saturn appears in your chart can suggest where you may feel inclined to pursue a career, because it shows us where we want to become an authority, and hard work often leads to mastery of the subject matter. Do not be intimidated by Saturn; instead, follow its guidance with enthusiasm and you'll be better for it.

Uranus

Uranus marks the first of the generational planets, otherwise known as outside planets. Uranus, Neptune, and Pluto travel at a rate much slower than the other planets, so their placement is consistent across an entire generation of humans. For example, most people born in the '90s have Pluto in Scorpio, so that entire generation has a Plutonian tilt to them. The same can be said for Uranus and Neptune. Uranus represents the need for innovation, variety and freedom. It rules Aquarius so wherever it falls in your chart shows where you might feel a desire to offer something to the larger collective, something unusual and inventive. It also shows in what areas you desire a lot of freedom.

For example, if you were born with Uranus in Libra, you might seem detached in your relationships because you value freedom in relationships. If it falls in Cancer, you might take an unorthodox approach to mothering.

Neptune

Neptune rules Pisces, and like Pisces, Neptune is hard to describe. Essentially, it represents all that is poetic and nuanced. It's often referred to as a higher octave of Venus, meaning it represents a sort of sacrificial/idealized love. Wherever Neptune falls in your natal chart shows the areas in which you have the propensity to lose yourself. If you have Neptune in Sagittarius, this might be in philosophy or adventure. If you have it in Scorpio, you may feel compelled to lose yourself in another person. Basically, Neptune, like Pisces, hates boundaries and wants to transcend.

Those with a really strong Neptune can easily fall into a victim/savior complex. This is why it's often referred to as the Jesus planet. There's a sacrificial element to it. Its presence also shows where we may tend toward confusion or disillusionment, or have poetic or artistic talents.

Pluto

Pluto is the last of the nine planets in our solar system. It's also the slowest of all the planets, so it's the most generational of the generationals. It rules Scorpio, so it has a dark and transformative energy. It represents the human need to come into contact with darkness and then transform through its presence. So wherever Pluto falls in your natal chart can indicate where you will endure challenges and battles.

Pluto also shows areas where you have a great deal of strength and willpower. It's often referred to as the survival planet. Whatever sign holds Pluto is where you have excellent survival instincts. It's also the planet of death and rebirth... trademark Scorpio stuff. If you have Pluto in a sign like Aries, you will experience the obsessive quality of Scorpio when it comes to starting projects or taking action. If you have it in Leo, you may be obsessed with how you come across to others.

RETROGRADES

Some of you, depending on your astrological knowledge, may have heard the term "retrograde." Retrogrades are often mentioned in mainstream because they are frequently seen. From an astronomical standpoint, a retrograde occurs when a planet appears to be moving backward from our vantage point here on earth. The planets don't actually move backward, but due to the earth's rotation, they appear to move backward when they're in retrograde. The symbolic effect is a feeling of chaos that asks us to rewind and reset.

If a planet was retrograding at the time of your birth, the expression of that planet may feel more jumbled than if it was not retrograding, otherwise referred to as "direct." When planets are direct, they are able to express themselves more naturally. When people complain about Mercury retrogrades, however, they usually aren't talking about their birth chart planet but in the context of transits, which will be explained next.

Transits

Transit is the word used to describe the current movement of the planets right at this moment. Transits are the means by which we often forecast future trends and developments. A transiting planet may pass over a point in a natal chart and then turn retrograde before going direct again, so this helps people who follow astrology to schedule doctor visits and other important appointments when there are no retrogrades. If you have an important surgery on Tuesday but Mercury is going into retrograde on Monday, you might fear that the doctor will lose your paperwork or something of that nature.

Since Mercury is the planet of communication, astrologers are especially cautious of its retrograde periods. The other planets retrograde less frequently and affect less important areas of life, so they don't receive as much attention. But every planet has its retrograde periods, and being aware of these periods can shed light on potential times of dysfunction.

Venus in Retrograde

When Venus is retrograding, the reset involves love and personal values. This is a time when it is wise to reflect on what you value most and why you value it. It can also be a good time to think about the type of people you're attracted to. Why do you find that type of person appealing? The same goes for clothing, art, or the recreational activities you engage in. Do you spend too much time drinking for pleasure and not enough time connecting with friends? Retrograding Venus could force you to become aware of these imbalances so you can make improvements when the planet goes direct again.

Mars in Retrograde

When Mars turns retrograde, our fighting spirit needs tweaking. This can bring a period when we feel like no matter how hard we try, our actions fail us. Since Mars is all about going after what you want, a retrograding Mars can bring frustration and cause stalemates. But it's also an opportunity to turn inward and consider why you're pursuing your particular goals. It can be a good time to adjust your course of action and alter your style of attack. Once Mars goes direct again, all your efforts will again have forward momentum. You can go after what you want in a direct way, which is exactly how Mars likes to function.

Jupiter in Retrograde

During Jupiter retrogrades, our need for meaning and expansion can take a pause. If you've been over-indulgent, this can be a period of sudden loss. Or if you're seeking more meaning and abundance, it can be a time for productive reflection or manifestation. Jupiter retrogrades often limit us in some way before expanding us once the retrograde is over. So the best way to make good use of a Jupiter retrograde phase is to think about where you want to expand and take appropriate measures to prepare for that expansion. For example, it's a good time to apply for a new job or scope out any classes you're thinking about taking.

Saturn in Retrograde

Saturn retrogrades can have the opposite effect of Jupiter. When Saturn is retrograding, it challenges our ability to discipline ourselves. Even if you're someone who finds it very easy to self-discipline, this can be a time when new limitations threaten your progress. The best way to handle a Saturn retrograde is by thinking about your restrictions and deciding if there is a better way to motivate yourself. Or, perhaps it's a good time for a break altogether.

Uranus in Retrograde

Uranus retrogrades can feel unsettling because Uranus is the planet of change. When you're in the midst of a Uranus transit, opportunities can pop up out of nowhere, but circumstances can also change for the worse all at once. Ultimately, though, Uranus changes things up to allow for more freedom, so when it's retrograding, your freedom may be curtailed during that time. But with a period of sudden restriction, you can find new and creative ways to achieve more freedom than you had before. Once Uranus goes direct, your life can open up in ways that you never would have imagined before the retrograde.

Neptune in Retrograde

Retrograding Neptune can bring plenty of confusion. Since it's the planet of transcendence but also disillusionment, it can make energy murky. It's a different kind of confusion from a Mercury retrograde, however. Mercury affects communication and travel, while Neptune affects more spiritual matters, such as love and connection. This means that when Neptune is retrograding, it can make arguments within relationships cloudy, like when you can't tell who is right and who is wrong. It can also be a time when you fall in love with the wrong person, only to realize afterward that they're bad news. Be especially cautious with retrograding Neptune. Things may not be clear until after the retrograde is over.

Pluto in Retrograde

When Pluto retrogrades, it often affects the whole collective more than the individuals within it. This is because Pluto is the outermost planet, so retrograding Pluto can cause things like political issues or even natural disasters. It can be a time when public secrets are revealed or power is taken away from an individual or group. Pluto's function is to destroy in order to be reborn, so retrograding Pluto can bring its fair share of battles. We may not even be conscious of these battles until Pluto has gone direct. Take notice when Pluto is almost finished retrograding. More often than not, you'll find a lot of turmoil affecting the entire collective during these times.

THE 12 HOUSES

The last piece of the natal chart puzzle is the houses. Again, the houses are distinguished by the tiny numbers surrounding the inner ring of the chart. These move counterclockwise, just like the signs, with the first house always located on the left side with the Ascendant. Each house relates in some way to the twelve signs of the zodiac. For example, since Aries is the first sign, the 1st house has an Aries tone to it. It's the house of identity, initiation, self-perception, and power. The 2nd house reflects the energy of Taurus, and so on through the signs in order.

The main difference between the houses and signs in a natal chart is the way the energies manifest. The signs will color the style of the planets' expressions, while the houses show what themes the planets will run into. For instance, if you have your natal Sun in Scorpio in the 7th house, you will shine as an individual by possessing Scorpio qualities and these qualities will show up most in your one-on-one relationships. (The 7th house is the house of one-on-one relationships). It's almost like the planets are the characters in a play, the signs are the costumes they wear, and the houses are the setting or the plot. If you have an abundance of planets in one house, a scenario known as a stellium, the themes of that house will be especially prevalent in your life. The planets naturally want to develop through whatever activities are associated with their house.

The 1st House

Now let's thoroughly explore each of the houses. The 1st house, as I've stated already, deals with Aries themes such as raw power of identity. If you have a lot of planets in the 1st house, identity will most likely be a major theme of your life. This can manifest in many ways, depending on the planets placed there. If you have Mars in the 1st house, for example, you'll have a great desire to assert yourself in a way that is unique to your individual identity. Asserting yourself will also come more naturally to you since it's a key element of your basic temperament.

The first house also deals with starting things, like initiating projects or taking action in general. It also deals with appearance, or how you present yourself, and the way you perceive yourself as an individual. The 1st house is the foundation of the zodiac, so its qualities are simple and straightforward. The more we progress through the chart, the more nuanced the houses become.

The 2nd House

The 2nd house relates to Taurus and deals with themes of security and values. If you have a 2nd house emphasis in your chart, building security will be one of the main themes in your psychological development. Security is a broad term, though. Depending on the individual, it can mean many different things. It can involve issues like creating financial security, but also can be about having strong political or social values, obtaining the material things you desire, etc. But if you have planets in the 2nd house, values, and building a meaningful life based on those values will act as a key life theme, whether those values are material, spiritual, social or political.

The 3rd House

The 3rd house is associated with the third sign, Gemini, so the themes are communication, travel, learning and language. It also involves siblings because Gemini is the symbolic twin of the zodiac and early schooling because the 3rd house highlights that feeling of being a child in grade school, when you're learning things for the first time and also how to interact with different personalities.

If you have planets in the 3rd house, activities such as learning, gossiping, and intellectualizing may prove especially fulfilling for you. Many writers and reporters, for example, have a 3rd house emphasis in their natal charts.

The 4th House

The 4th house is Cancer's house and it always falls on the bottom of the chart, near the IC (Imum Coeli, which is Latin for "bottom of the sky"). The IC is the "home point" of the chart, so it says a lot about what makes us feel cozy and at home. This house is a bit more complex than the previous ones. It deals with themes of ancestry, family, childhood upbringing, home, emotional nurturance, mothering and inner-thought processes.

If you have a 4th house emphasis, any number of these themes will be important in your life. Your family or heritage may be of special importance, or you may use your imagination to create art. It's likely that your mother will be a significant figure in your life and learning how to nurture yourself emotionally may be a major life obstacle.

The 5th House

The 5th house rules Leo and deals with themes like creativity, hobbies, self-expression, romance and fun in general. To be honest, the 5th house is all about connecting to our inner child, the playful and authentic part of yourself that is unique to you as an individual. Having fun and being playful is one of the main ways to connect with your inner-child.

If you have a lot of planets in the 5th house, authenticity and fun will be some of the trademarks of your life. People with a strong 5th house need to discover their passions and express themselves through those passions. Ultimately, it's all about self-love and enjoying life.

The 6th House

The 6th house is Virgo's house, so it's more work-related than any of the previous ones. It shows how we approach work, our daily habits, our health, and our bodies. Many people with a strong 6th house turn out to be health nuts or take organization very seriously. Additionally, whatever planets fall in your 6th will say a lot about the way you go about work.

If you have Mars in the 6th, you'll have a strong desire to approach work your own way, rather than anyone else's. If you have Mercury, you may need a lot of socializing time at work. Fundamentally, though, the 6th house is about the mind-body-spirit connection. With a strong 6th, you'll want to create routines and rituals that support the mind-body relationship.

The 7th House

The 7th house always falls on the right side of the chart at the Descendant. If the Ascendant shows how we perceive and present ourselves to the world, the Descendant shows how others reflect our inherent perceptions. It's the house of Libra, and deals with one-on-one relationships. This includes partnerships, friendships, romantic relationships and marriage.

If you have a lot of planets in the 7th, your relationships will probably be extremely important to you. More than that, though, your relationships will constantly teach you new things about yourself. Whatever people you attract in your life act as a mirror for you to learn more about yourself. That's why people with strong 7th houses often end up being people-pleasers--they're honed in on the people around them.

The 8th House

The 8th house is the house of Scorpio so it's one of the more intense houses of the zodiac. The 8th takes the themes of the 7th and amps them up a notch. Relationships are also a theme here, but not just any relationships - intimate ones. The 8th house is where we learn about ourselves through transformation, and this usually involves transforming through intimacy.

The most stereotypical expression of this house is a love for sex and psychology—something that delves beyond superficial relationships. It's also the house of shared assets, financial inheritance, death and divorce. It often deals with heavy topics, so people who have planets in the 8th tend to be very wise. They like to see life from below the surface and they're not afraid to get their hands dirty.

The 9th House

The 9th house is the house of Sagittarius, so it deals with expansion, adventure, higher learning and travel. It's also the house of in-laws. These different themes may seem un-related, but when you think about Sagittarius, it makes sense. Sagittarius craves meaning and growth. Activities like travel and higher learning provide that.

In-laws represent a sort of expanded family, where you learn about the upbringing and culture of another couple in an intimate way. People with a strong 9th house usually enjoy travel and some enjoy mind-expanding activities like drugs. It is also said that the 9th house reveals something about how we interpret God--again, "meaning" being a key signature.

The 10th House

The 10th house rules Capricorn and it falls at the top of the chart with the MC, or midheaven. Both the midheaven and the 10th house say a lot about what you desire from your career or your public reputation. It can also mean that your father, or how you go about fathering yourself, will play a vital role in your life.

If you have a lot of planets in your 10th house, you're most likely ambitious and perhaps a little power-hungry. With a strong 10th, you may strive to be an authority in some way, and your career pursuits will most likely reflect that. This house also shows how you relate to the public and how the public perceives you. If you have Neptune in the 10th, for example, you may have a very compassionate and emotional public persona. If you have the Sun, you'll probably wish to shine in the public in some way.

The 11th House

The 11th house piggy-backs off the 10th because it deals with themes of public contribution. While the 10th is more about career and public reputation, the 11th is about contribution to society. We all have an urge to leave something significant behind us, something that will help the larger community of which we are a part. This is the essence of the 11th house.

It also deals with hopes, dreams and wishes. It's the house of Aquarius, so friendship and communities play a vital role for 11th house individuals. If you have many planets here, you'll want to offer something to whatever groups you belong. You may even have the potential to create something truly inventive that will help foster the growth of the human collective.

The 12th House

The 12th house is the most nuanced and complicated of all houses. It deals with themes like transcendence, imagination, meditation, creativity, death, rebirth, and escapism. In fact, escapism might be the key word. If you have a lot of planets in the 12th, you'll feel a connection to the rest of life and humanity in a way that is far more intense than other people. It can feel a lot like existential dread, because you're constantly questioning your purpose in life.

It's also common for people with a 12th house emphasis to crave experiences that encapsulate a feeling of deep belonging. Many of these people love to get involved in a church community, for example, but if you take escapism too far, you can easily wind up in institutions like hospitals, jails, or rehab facilities. Just like Pisces, 12th house people need to transcend, and drugs and alcohol are one way of doing that. Mostly, though, an abundance of planets in the 12th house means you have great empathy for all of humanity, as well as a vivid imagination.

Now that you have a basic understanding of the planets, signs, and houses, you are well on your way to interpreting a natal chart on your own. Remember that chart interpretation requires a bit of creativity. There are always many planets and energies to consider when analyzing your personality and life patterns. You may have the same exact Mars placement as your best friend, and yet the expression manifests differently because you have different Sun signs, or perhaps your Mars is next to Venus while theirs is opposite Pluto.

When you get more in-depth, you'll see that each of the planets has a relationship with the others, and these are called aspects. Aspects are shown by the red and blue lines on the chart that connect the planets, and they reveal much about the tension or ease that the different parts of your personality contain. That's more advanced stuff, though. For now, start by getting a feel for the planets and houses. Generate your own natal chart online and Google what your different planet placements mean. You'll be surprised how complex and specific the descriptions are, but this reflects how complex and specific all humans are.

4

THE SUN SIGNS

Since the Sun signs are the most important, and most widely recognized component of astrology, we'll discuss them more in-depth. Plus, with accurate knowledge of the Sun signs, you'll be better able to interpret planets and houses, because they all go back to the Sun signs. For instance, if you understand the energy of Aries, you can then apply it to the 1st house since the 1st house is Aries' house and also to Mars, since Mars is Aries' planet.

ARIES

Element: Fire
Planet: Mars
House: 1st
Dates: March 21–April 19

Aries is the first sign and it's a fire sign, which means it's all about raw power. Many famous athletes are Aries because they have so much masculine energy that requires some sort of outlet. Like fire, Aries is reactive. It's not a sign that carefully ponders, it prefers immediate action. It also has a strong desire to feel special and important. All three fire signs have that quality, but with Aries, it's almost a secret desire to feel like a superhero. Since assertive Mars is Aries' ruling planet, Aries people love going to battle, either through sports, fighting for an underdog, or being overcome by things like road rage. The typical energy of an Aries personality is energetic, blunt, assertive, excitable, and sometimes loud.

Sometimes, Aries can also be aggressive. Many people who are attracted to joining the military tend to be

Aries--it gives them an opportunity to discover their power and feel like a hero. No matter what career or interests Aries pursues, they tend to attack it with full force. Aries needs to stay constantly busy and working toward something, otherwise, life is incredibly dull. It's also worth noting that Aries resembles the qualities of its planet, Mars. Mars is a fiery red planet, often associated with masculinity, and the Aries personality reflects those qualities.

Aries is the first sign, so it's the most straightforward of all the zodiac. It's the least likely to react one way while feeling a different way. It doesn't need to play games or hide behind layers of complicated psychology in order to function in society. There's a kind of fearlessness associated with Aries. These people have a great deal of energy, and they tend to have lofty goals as well. They need to stay busy, and to have plenty of excitement and things to do, so most are very determined individuals, working relentlessly to reach their desired goals. They can be pushy, and sometimes crass. But they know how to have fun and live a life full of passion.

TAURUS

Element: Earth
Planet: Venus
House: 2nd
Dates: April 20-May 20

In contrast to Aries, Taurus is slow, preferring to ground itself through the appreciation of earthly comforts. While Aries is out fighting to get ahead in life, Taurus is sitting on the couch enjoying its favorite movie with an expensive blanket. All three earth signs are sensory, but Venus-ruled Taurus is especially attuned to appreciating the physical. In fact, Taurus tends to build its life around accumulating things that offer physical comfort. What that physical comfort entails, however, depends on the individual and their personal values. One Taurus may be obsessed with clothes, spending less on food so they have more for shoes, while another may love cars or books. Many have passionate political beliefs. And they tend to have a great sense of humor, which is based on their logical view of the world. Jerry Seinfeld, for instance, is a

Taurus who's made a career out of pointing out how absurd everyday life is.

Since Taurus is ruled by Venus, these people also have a need for pleasure and beauty. They tend to have the best taste of any of the zodiac signs because they know the difference between quality and mediocrity. They have an inherent sense of aesthetic beauty and often make great artists and designers. The downside to the Taurus personality is that they can become rigid or overly set in their ways. On the flip side, though, they're excellent at following through on things without letting obstacles derail them.

Taurus is known for its soft and gentle disposition, but if you try to push Taureans into doing something they don't want to do, you may face backlash. As the 2nd sign of the zodiac, Taurus is simplistic, much like Aries. It knows what it likes and it knows what it wants. This is their most admirable quality, but if Taurus becomes too greedy or selfish, things can become dark.

Sometimes, it's hard for Tauruses to compromise. They feel they have a special relationship with their values, so it's difficult when they're expected to value something else instead. Think of a future bride planning out her wedding, but then taking things overboard and becoming so demanding that she's now a Bridezilla. But, we all have a lot to learn from Taureans' deep appreciation of values and aesthetics. Their stubbornness can be endearing once you get to know them.

GEMINI

Element: Air
Planet: Mercury
House: 3rd
Dates: May 21-June 20

Much like a curious child, Gemini is a notorious troublemaker, which sometimes makes them appear immature. Really, though, Gemini is an expert at communication who isn't afraid to tell it like it is. They don't take life too seriously and possess a quick wit that can dazzle more introverted signs. Sarcasm and wordplay come easily to these people. There's a playful, mischievous energy with them and they love to learn and debate. They also love to ask a lot of questions. For a Gemini, the more information they have, the more they can impress people at parties and also stimulate their own minds.

Geminis become bored very quickly without a surplus of new and interesting information. They also love gossip and trash-talking. Since Gemini is ruled by Mercury, these individuals have a mercurial tilt to their personalities. They love variety, like taking short trips to meet new and interesting people. And they love to solve puzzles or other complicated intellectual matters. The negative traits associated with Gemini have to do with lack of groundedness. Gemini wants to constantly explore new terrain. Unlike Taurus, it hates being fixed to one thing. This can make Gemini appear two-faced or inauthentic.

It's easy to catch Gemini in a lie because they'll often say one thing one day and something different the next. But this is because their opinions are rarely set in stone. They enjoy changing their mind and seeing things through new perspectives. Geminis are also expert chameleons and they know how to be "the cool one" in any crowd. This can make others feel like they never see the authentic person underneath all that. But Gemini is an avid explorer, and too fluid to stick to a single identity. Gemini simply loathes being confined to a box. If you accept Gemini for what it is, you can enjoy the fun, cerebral, and unpredictable energy it brings. You'll also laugh a lot if you're willing to engage in their clever antics.

CANCER

Element: Water
Planet: Moon
House: 4th
Dates: June 21-July 22

Cancer is the first of the water signs so it's known for being emotional and moody. Some Cancer men are very artistic, using their emotions to give birth to something as a mother births a child. These people can make amazing chefs, gardeners, or home builders. No matter what the outlet, Cancer needs to nurture. Having kids and raising a family is often very important to them too. Many are also excellent comedians, using their emotions in their humor. Since Cancer is ruled by the moon, these people tend toward emotional extremes. Things that might seem insignificant to others can cause a hyper-sensitive reaction, but they're also excellent at comforting others because they understand more than most the ups and downs of life. It's important that Cancers embrace their emotions and the shifts that come with them, but some repress them, much like their symbol, the crab, which moves sideways.

Family is often extremely important to Cancers. If something is keeping them from having a close relationship with their own family, then it is extremely important that they form a solid family through friends or marriage. Most Cancers also love pets because they get to nurture them as they would a child. Mothering is what they're meant to do, whether they do it in a masculine way by raising a large dog, or a feminine way by raising a child. Regardless, Cancer needs living things to nurture. They make great romantic partners for this reason. Just be prepared for those mood swings.

LEO

Element: Fire
Planet: Sun
House: 5th
Dates: July 23-August 22

Leo is ruled by the Sun, so as I stated earlier, it loves to shine. It also radiates warmth--a generous and loving quality that comes from wanting to feel good and make others feel good as well. It's no surprise, then, that confidence is a huge theme for Leos. Although they're stereotypically known as the performers of the zodiac, many Leos are quite shy. This is why confidence is key. It's Leo's journey in life to understand itself and express itself through that understanding.

Like Aries, Leo also has a deep desire to feel special, but it's not a heroic kind of special that Leo craves. Rather, Leo wants to feel unique and larger than life. This is why many Leos become artists. Art helps them get in touch with their authenticity and express it through a specific medium. Leos also have a child-like quality to them. They tend to be playful and they're always in search of fun.

Because of this trait, they can party harder than any other sign. They love to feel alive, like the Sun shining bright. Drugs and alcohol are a way to achieve that sensation, but so is letting loose with friends. It's no surprise that Leo loves romance more than any other sign. They love to date and fall in love because this allows them to bask in the glow of their specialness. Another quality about Leo that is rarely mentioned harkens to its similarities with Aquarius (its opposite): Leos enjoy trying to understand the human experience. Many love astrology and psychology because these disciplines allow them to understand themselves and the people around them. It's a more introspective sign than many realize.

VIRGO

Element: Earth
Planet: Mercury
House: 6th
Dates: August 23–September 22

♍

Virgo shares its ruling planet, Mercury, with Gemini, though Virgo and Gemini have very different energies. Gemini is all over the place, while Virgo is more grounded and consistent. Still, Virgo has a knack for understanding all the tiny pieces that make up the puzzle. They're also good with language. And since Virgo's energy is earthy and logical, it has a talent for using its mercurial talents toward physical endeavors. Many music producers are Virgos because they're so good at layering sounds and editing. It makes sense that many rappers are Geminis, while the people making the beats are Virgos. Virgos also strive to be perfect in every way possible - again, because they're master editors. They need to be cautious of this though because perfection is obviously impossible. This is also why Virgos are great critics. They have the best critical lens of all the zodiac signs because of how detail-oriented they are.

Because they're the sign of the physical body, these are the people who need sex more than those of any other sign. Many porn stars and sex addicts are Virgos. Many Virgos go to great lengths to take care of their bodies and overall health. Another, more wholesome, quality that Virgo possesses is its need to serve, because it's not a sign that can be selfish. Virgos are at their best when they're helping others, and their careers often involve this in some capacity.

LIBRA

Element: Air
Planet: Venus
House: 7th
Dates: September 23-October 22

Libra shares a planet with Taurus, but it's an air sign so, like Virgo with Gemini, its energy is different from that of Taurus. Both are Venus-ruled, so both have a special connection to the concept of beauty. But Libras are obsessed with beauty in a way that is different from Taurus, perhaps because Libra is a relationship sign. It's one of the signs most concerned with its physical appearance. Many Libras tend to be gym rats or women who need routine manicures. Libra is also the only sign in the zodiac to have an inanimate object – the scales - as its symbol. This suggests something about the nature of Libra's personality--it has to stay detached in order to weigh options and achieve balance.

What is interesting about Libra is that, although it presents itself as a positive, upbeat personality, it can quickly turn negative. This reinforces the concept of the scale; Libras need to achieve a healthy balance of harmony with others while achieving their goals, otherwise they can become irritable.

Ultimately, Libras want to infuse the world with as much beauty as possible. They love to fight for a cause and fight against injustice. Like Cancer, many Libras love animals and they often have many pets because they have a desire to care for those who can't care for themselves. They love to help others. But they will expect praise for their efforts! Libras need to feel appreciated, especially in romantic relationships. They're very talkative and often bubbly.

SCORPIO

Element: Water
Planet: Pluto
House: 8th
Dates: October 23-November 21

Scorpio is the sex addict or therapist of the zodiac. It's ruled by dark and cold Pluto, so it craves intimacy above all else. For this reason, Scorpio is probably the strongest sign mentally and emotionally. Many Scorpios have been through dark times in their lives, which is part of the reason they tend to embrace darkness as adults. Many of those into astrology talk about how "evil" or grudge-holding Scorpios can be, but few talk about the power of this sign and the theme of transformation that's at the core of the personality. It's as if Scorpios attract dark forces that demand they evolve into something new.

If you know any Scorpios well, you'll probably notice that they've had their fair share of drama in life; drama that has changed them on a cellular level. It's no wonder, then, that their symbol is a scorpion, because it has a stinger. They're strong enough that their emotions spill out spontaneously, unlike Cancer and Pisces, but they still feel deeply.

Some Scorpios build a wall around themselves and are perceived as brooding. They know that vulnerability can be used against them, so many over-protect themselves. This is counter-productive, of course, because Scorpio craves intimacy. And in order to achieve true intimacy, we all need to be vulnerable. Still, Scorpios feel everything, and excel at feeling what's going on underneath the surface of any situation. They make great criminal investigators or even life insurance salespeople. They're strong enough to enter fields that deal with death because they're all too familiar with the cyclical nature of life.

SAGITTARIUS

Element: Fire
Planet: Jupiter
House: 9th
Dates: November 22-December 21

Sagittarius is the final fire sign, so it's reactive and excitable but in a slightly more "mature" way. It's ruled by the largest planet, Jupiter, so this affects the disposition. They want life to be grand, expansive, adventurous and full. The bigger the better with Sagittarius. Sagittarius has a tendency to go too far with things. Of all the signs, they're the most likely to become extremists. At the same time, their optimism combined with their larger-than-life personalities inspire and excite others. And since Sagittarius also craves truth and meaning, these are the people most likely to get high on psychedelics and hypothesize about the meaning of life.

They are also straight shooters, only interested in the truth, just like their opposite, Gemini. Both have a sarcastic, quick-witted sense of humor. Sagittarians make great interviewers and comedians. They're always looking for answers and they know how to talk. They may cut you off a lot, but it's usually welcomed because they're so funny.

Sagittarius can have difficulty staying on one track and disciplining itself. Its planet, Jupiter, is the opposite of the focused Saturn. But there's a reason why Sagittarius's symbol is the centaur with a bow and arrow. It needs to focus in on a target while remaining wild and free like a horse. It's a constant balancing act, much like Libra has. But if Sagittarius has core philosophies or "truths" to lean on, they have a better chance of achieving that balance. If they can expand through the mind, they won't have to expand through material things, in which case they won't let their wandering spirit get the best of them.

CAPRICORN

Element: Earth
Planet: Saturn
House: 10th
Dates: December 21-January 20

Capricorn is one of the more serious signs. Although, all the Earth signs have a secret golden sense of humor. Nevertheless, with Saturn as its ruling planet, Capricorn has an inner-critic that makes ambitiousness and security two of its main priorities. It's known as the father of the zodiac because it's very concerned with "bread-winning" and achieving success. These are the worry-warts of the zodiac. With so much focus on the future, they can't help but fear the inevitable obstacles. And since security is a priority, their fears often revolve around this issue. Needless to say, Capricorn is the most responsible of all the signs.

Sometimes, though, you'll get a Capricorn who resents this and decides to live as a rebel. But when the Saturn Return strikes at around twenty-eight years old (this is when Saturn returns to the exact place in the zodiac that it was when you were born), they realize that society needs them to be responsible and become more willing to take on those responsibilities. Saturn Returns are a big deal for Capricorn because Saturn is its ruling planet.

Because of their inherent responsible natures, Capricorns make great leaders and tend to aim for positions of authority. Many politicians, as well as entrepreneurs and business leaders, are Capricorns. They thrive when they are in positions of authority. That could mean being an expert on their own niche topic or serving as the leader of a team. Capricorns are dependable, and while they do get anxious, they're easy to talk to and are incredibly down to earth. They may dip out of the party early, but they'll have the best advice when you're suffering from a hangover the next day. They're a good friend to have.

AQUARIUS

Element: Air
Planet: Uranus
House: 11th
Dates: January 21-February 18

The last air sign, Aquarius is the rebel, artist, mediator, and often "weirdo." It's common for Aquarians to feel like outsiders for this reason, but they often prefer it this way. The paradox, though, is that Aquarius is also the sign of group consciousness. It wants to belong but it also wants to be unique. This is why many Aquarians are inventors or artists. When they pursue these activities, they are able to use their uniqueness to provide something useful for humanity at large. At worst,

Aquarians are detached and sometimes even robotic. More than any other sign, they have the propensity to intellectualize instead of feel, which can annoy their significant others for obvious reasons.

Aquarius has a gift for noticing patterns, which is what makes them great innovators--they can observe things on a broad scope, spot consistencies, and then offer their own unique interpretation. Isaac Newton was an Aquarius, and so was psychologist Carl Jung. Since Aquarians have a special interest in humanity, many pursue fields like psychology. Others show their appreciation for humanity through art or non-profit work. But since Aquarius is also deeply intellectual, it needs to find things that challenge the mind. Many enjoy discussing topics with friends, especially since friendships mean a lot to Aquarius. Its symbol is the water bearer, so it's meant to offer something to the collective, whether that refers to their friend group, their peers at work, or the world as a whole. If you're facing challenges in a group situation, bring an Aquarius in to act as a diplomat. This is their special skill.

PISCES

Element: Water
Planet: Neptune

House: 12th
Dates: February 19-March 20

Pisces is the final and possibly the most complicated sign in astrology. Because it arrives at the end of the zodiac, it represents the end, as well as the beginning of a new cycle. Therefore, it's less rigid than the other signs. If you know any Pisces, you have probably seen first-hand how they seem to lack a filter. Pisces is the sign of zero boundaries. They want to connect and feel like they are never separate from others. Because Pisces has such a deep connection to their own feelings as well as those of others, they're naturally gifted at poetry, music, storytelling, and all things imaginative.

They can also be cry-babies or have anger issues. Unlike Scorpio, Pisces has little self-control. If they feel something, they'll express it. They're sort of like a sponge. They take everything in and then they let it seep out. Many Pisces are doctors or healers of some kind because this allows them to care for others, which comes naturally to them. Many actors or musicians are also Pisces.

Pisces is the most mystical sign of the zodiac. Most Pisces are spiritual in some way because they can intuitively feel how all of life is interconnected. This is why they're also natural empaths. However, some Pisces can be emotionally immature. If a Pisces doesn't actively try to achieve some level of self-awareness, they may find themselves having tantrums. Since they function like an emotional sponge, they have to create strong boundaries to keep their heads on straight. This is difficult because Pisces hates boundaries. It would rather blend with everyone else than keep its emotions separate. But if Pisces practices self-awareness, it can be an extremely empathetic and comforting presence to be around.

5

ASTROLOGY AND RELATIONSHIPS

Astrology is an excellent way to understand others. When you look at another person's birth chart or even just discover their "big 3," which is someone's Sun, Moon and Ascendant placement, you get an insight into their unique psyche. This can help you relate to others. Just knowing that someone you're talking to is a fire sign versus a water sign can affect the way you choose to interact with them.

If you're talking to a fire sign, for example, you might benefit from a blunt approach. If you're dealing with a water sign, you'll want to practice sensitivity. If you're speaking to an Earth sign, be realistic. And when you're talking to an Air sign, you should try to keep things intellectual but light. Each personality reacts differently to various styles of communication. Learning which style works most efficiently for which sign will help you determine the best communication approach for that person.

It's important to understand your own natal chart and your own psychology as well, of course. Once you have a clear grasp on why you communicate the way you do, you can learn how to alter your approach depending on the other person or circumstance. But if you don't first understand yourself, it's very hard to adjust your communication style with others.

Astrology shows us why we attract the people we do, and what we're meant to learn from them. It also shows the unique energies behind relationship dynamics and then presents these energies in an objective way. There's no other tool in the world that allows for that kind of insight, so it's an amazing mechanism for understanding what lies at the heart of relationships. More importantly, though, it shows how we can get the most out of our partnerships. It can mean the difference between thriving in a relationship or beating one's head against the wall. Even more good news; there are several different methods within astrology that allow you to explore relationship dynamics. Chart comparison is a major one. So let's talk about Synastry and Composite charts.

Synastry Charts

There are a few very specific ways to explore relationships through astrology. One is through a synastry chart. A synastry chart basically overlaps two natal charts, so you can see how the two charts interact. You can generate synastry charts for free on many astrology websites. If you want to see how the houses line up, though, you'll need the birth times of both parties involved. Once you have accurate birth information, and you generate a synastry chart online, you can interpret the way the two charts interact by observing the outer and inner circles.

You'll notice that your partner's Mars may fall into your 5th house, and it may even fall right next to your Sun. This would suggest that your partner's assertive energy can help you express yourself. It can also mean that they challenge your ego expression. Carefully observing the synastry contacts will help you to form a detailed analysis of how your planets interact with one another.

Composite Charts

A composite chart, on the other hand, will show you how your relationship functions as its own entity. Composite charts are easier to interpret because they look exactly like a normal birth chart. A composite chart is derived by calculating the midpoint between both people's planetary positions and points to create a whole new chart. By doing this, you can see the combined energy and the combined potential of your partnership. If you're curious whether your relationship has a more profound purpose, a composite chart is a good thing to investigate. It's also great for understanding how others may perceive you as a unit.

The best and easiest way to use astrology for relationship purposes, though, is simply by examining the two birth charts and getting a feel for what each chart needs and how it operates. Keep in mind that we often need and attract what we lack in ourselves, i.e. the concept that opposites attract. At the same time, too much of one thing can create boredom. Astrology teaches us that good relationships have an equal balance of opposites and similarities. This is just one thing to consider when comparing the energies of two natal charts.

In terms of relating to others, and understanding everyone's unique and specific energies, let's now explore each of the Sun signs, as well as their corresponding houses. This will give you an idea of what to expect when you're trying to improve a relationship based on the other person's sign.

SUN IN ARIES OR SUN IN THE 1ST HOUSE

Aries individuals are fiery, probably the fieriest of all the zodiac signs. This has both pros and cons. If you enjoy the straight-shooter type, then you'll get on fine with Aries. But when dealing with an Aries, you have to understand that the intensity of their reactions doesn't always equal the intensity of their core feelings. Like fire, they have to burn, but then they quickly fizzle out. If you're used to communicating more sensitively, Aries' lack of a filter could easily rub you the wrong way. The benefit, though, is that you always know where you stand with an Aries.

Other signs may keep their feelings to themselves in order to maintain harmony, but with Aries, you often know what they're thinking and feeling because they'll come right out and say it. If they have a Libra moon, they may try to foster harmony, of course, but normally, Aries prefers blunt honesty over sugarcoating or lying to keep the peace. Aries love to get excited and have fun. If you want to appeal to an Aries, engage with them in a fun activity that requires some energy - anything physical is a good idea.

When communicating with someone who has the Sun in their 1st house, understand that identity is a key theme. You don't want to say or do anything that threatens a 1st house Sun's identity. Instead, you want to lift them up and make them aware of their individual skills and talents. These people love to learn new things about themselves, so make sure to compliment them and help them discover their unique selves. Additionally, these people need lots of freedom to initiate projects and spontaneously start new things. Make sure you don't thwart their energy. Encourage them and they'll be forever grateful and motivated.

SUN IN TAURUS OR SUN IN THE 2ND HOUSE

Taurus has a reputation for stubbornness. They can become especially upset when things don't go according to plan. So when you're communicating with a Taurus, make sure you know your plan ahead of time and that you communicate it thoroughly, and *then* stick to it. There's nothing Taureans hate more than expecting one thing but getting another, so with Taurus, consistency is everything.

It's also important to remember that Taurus is incredibly logic-based. They're very sensual, but not necessarily romantic. Their love language is gift-giving. They love to receive tangible things of value. If your behavior is chaotic or unpredictable, it might make Taurus feel uncomfortable. Taurus people are stubborn as hell. They need a lot of time to come around to opinions that contradict their own. If you're patient, though, you can get through to them and have a stable, long-lasting partnership. They'll always be a rock for you to lean on, so try to offer the same in return.

When dealing with a 2nd house Sun, understand that security is a high priority in life. This can take many forms, but most often it means they need to acquire a decent amount of money and establish roots before they can freely give themselves to another person. The best thing you can do for a 2nd house partner is help them build the security they crave. Help them save money and apply for jobs, or help them renovate their home. These are the ways they feel supported in a partnership. And do whatever you can to lift their self-esteem. Self-esteem is strongly linked to their values and security, so remind them how impressed you are with the life they've built for themselves.

SUN IN GEMINI OR SUN IN THE 3RD HOUSE

Unlike Taurus, Gemini thrives on a bit of chaos. So much so that they may actively try to infuse chaos into your relationship through mischief and spontaneity. To communicate with a Gemini, be sure to provide lots of details and be ready for plenty of questions. Geminis are endlessly curious. They're like the journalists of the zodiac, always looking for the next fun gossip and exciting news to share.

If you want to keep a Gemini engaged, make sure you have plenty of interesting information to give them. They love bizarre stories and anecdotes about people in their lives. Also maintain a sense of humor, since this is not a sign that prefers deep conversation. Instead, charm them with your colorful anecdotes and strong opinions. Be ready to debate with them and to be on the receiving end of sarcasm. You should also know that Gemini loves playing devil's advocate. When you raise a topic, be ready for a debate. This doesn't mean they won't see your side - they simply enjoy arguing.

When dealing with a 3rd house individual, understand that they need lots of room to explore new ideas and the immediate environment is often their playground. These people tend to talk a great deal and jump from one subject to the next. They might also go off on tangents, then be distracted by something else before returning to the tangent. They're honed in on their thoughts as well as their environment. It's easy for them to stay in the present moment and remain spontaneous. These people are often anxious and bored at all hours of the day, so try to keep the immediate environment engaging and stimulating.

SUN IN CANCER OR SUN IN THE 4TH HOUSE

Cancers are very different from their three predecessors. Cancer is emotional and nurturing, which means that communication with them needs to contain those qualities. Many Cancers have a good sense of humor, and others prefer to deflect through humor, but don't let them fool you--they're incredibly sensitive. It's no surprise that they appreciate people who communicate in a warm and caring way. Sometimes you won't even know you offended a Cancer until much later, when you hear about it from someone else. You have to be understanding of Cancer's emotional quirks. They want to be nurtured more than anything, but they're also excellent at nurturing others, so it's well worth it to provide the steady love they need.

Fourth house people have unique relationships to family and heritage. Depending on whether or not the Sun is involved, they may have close relationships with their family, or the opposite may be true. Either way, the family will be a shaping agent and an important theme in their personal development. People with the Sun in the 4th house need to create their own family that feels solid and secure. If you're in a relationship with one of these people, building a close family needs to be a priority. Whether big or small, these people need to feel connected to others in a familial way. The physical home is also a major source of comfort. So if you live with a 4th house person, be sure to keep the home cozy. Your 4th house partner will shower you with love in return.

SUN IN LEO OR SUN IN THE 5TH HOUSE

Leos are easy to have relationships with because they love being in love more than any other sign. Many people complain about Leos' tendency toward egotistical behavior, but it's just because Leos know better than the rest of the zodiac how to love themselves. And since they say you can't really love another until you love yourself, Leo is a step ahead.

In general, they tend to exude warmth and pride, which are attractive qualities when you're forming a relationship with someone. Whether shy or extroverted, Leos need plenty of room to shine, though, and they need space for their fantastical dreams to run wild. Make sure you give them that space. They like to have fun and feel important. As long as you can support them in that, they'll make you feel important as well. Ask them a lot of questions about themselves and lift them up. They'll usually reciprocate.

Fifth house people need to express themselves. If they can't, they can become depressed. In many ways, you need to play the role of devoted audience member to your 5th house partner. You also need to engage in play with them, because 5th house people are children at heart. They need a partner who will embrace fun activities and hobbies. These individuals are constantly striving for authenticity, so as a partner, you need to encourage their authentic expression. Don't try to turn them into someone they're not. It will never work.

SUN IN VIRGO OR SUN IN THE 6TH HOUSE

Virgos also enjoy relationships, and they generally make good, reliable partners. They're very helpful and love to take good, practical care of the people around them. If you're not as logically-minded as Virgo, though, you could run into problems in your interactions with them. It can be hard to get Virgo to look at things in more nuanced ways. If you're a Pisces or Aquarius, a conflict of worldviews could ensue. Also know that Virgo takes its health and routines seriously. If you want to get along well with a Virgo, you should support them in their rituals. They're very calm, and they tend to embrace all personalities, but they're not shy about offering their two cents. If don't value constructive criticism, you'll need to get over that when dealing with a Virgo.

Sixth house people are all about their rituals. They have a specific way they prefer to go about their daily routines, and as a partner, you need to be supportive of this. Every 6th house person has different rituals, of course, but the point is that routine is important. These people also tend to pay special attention to their bodies and overall health. Don't be surprised if your 6th house partner wants you to go to the gym with them, or enroll in a weekly yoga class. Embrace their mind-body connection and you can learn a great deal about appreciating the little things in life.

SUN IN LIBRA OR SUN IN THE 7TH HOUSE

Libras are the ultimate relationship sign. They love to be in a partnership because it makes them feel more balanced and whole. They also value harmony, so they will go out of their way to check in with you and make sure that everything is peaceful. But if Libra becomes an extreme people-pleaser, the pendulum may swing, turning them into someone who wants to be pleasant but is unable to because they are filled with resentment. If you're interested in pursuing a relationship with a Libra, make sure you have open communication, and that they're willing to address the good, the bad, and the ugly. Some Libras prefer to sweep the ugly under the rug, and then it might emerge in passive-aggressive ways. But beyond all that, Libra is a generous and lovely sign that has an ample amount of love to share with the world.

Seventh house people are a unique breed. Relationships are more important to them than they are for others because they need relationships to learn more about themselves and develop into a fully-formed human being. For 7th house people, relationships are the means through which they learn about themselves, so they're almost like mirrors. Be aware of the psychological significance at play in these relationships. Many 7th house relationships feel fated. You might be perceived by them as being their other half, completing them in some way. This kind of projection is common with 7th house people. And while harmony is a priority with these people, fights and disagreements are inevitable. Just make sure you're not the product of your partner's projection, and that you maintain your own identity.

SUN IN SCORPIO OR SUN IN THE 8TH HOUSE

Scorpios are amazing partners if you crave a deep and intimate connection. If you're interested in dating a Scorpio, don't expect a superficial love affair. They need something deep and transformative. If you're not willing to explore the depths with them, the relationship will never work. Instead, you'll see the jealous, stubborn, grudge-holding side of Scorpio. But if you crave something deep, where you both touch each other's souls and transform through the relationship, a Scorpio is the ideal partner. They feel intensely and they love intensely. It can feel amazing to be the object of Scorpio's desires because when they're in love, they're obsessed. But beware of the potential for power struggles and unregistered emotions. With Scorpio, it's best to lay everything out on the table, address emotions as they come up, and maintain the passionate electricity.

Eighth house people carry a similar energy to Scorpios. They crave deep, soulful connections, where both partners are almost combined as one. This can get messy, of course, but 8th house Suns kind of like it that way. In order to be truly intimate, you have to be willing to get your hands dirty. Obviously, if you're intimidated by that kind of deep connection, an 8th house person is not the right partner for you. These people tend to like astrology because they're interested in anything that delves beneath the surface layer of things. They also love to uncover mysteries and hypothesize about spirituality. If you enjoy topics like these, an 8th house partner will constantly stimulate your mind. Also, they love sex, so that's a bonus!

SUN IN SAGITTARIUS OR SUN IN THE 9TH HOUSE

Sagittarians are also passionate people, but they operate differently than Scorpios. Sagittarius is passionate about life in general. It needs to expand and find meaning through love. If you want to form a relationship with one, be prepared to go on adventures together. You'll need to infuse spontaneity into the relationship and be ready for random outings and trips to the yoga studio. Many Sagittarians, whether they're aware of it or not, need a lot of space in their relationships. They don't like to feel tied down, and need to roam free. You'll also have to be prepared for lots of intellectual and philosophical conversations, along with a bit of sarcasm. Gossip with them, and they'll be grateful.

Ninth house people are similar to Sagittarians in that they need adventure and freedom. Some pursue this through the mind, such as through mind-expanding drugs or writing. Others love to travel to foreign places at least once a year. They love conversations about broad topics like the meaning of life. Some may have an important relationship with God or religion. In-laws can also play an important role in the lives of 9th house people. They also tend to enjoy reading and learning, but only about specific subjects. The 9th house manifests in many different ways, but one thing's for sure: these people need adventure and expansion. If you're a homebody, a 9th house partner may result in a lot of resentment from both parties.

SUN IN CAPRICORN OR SUN IN THE 10TH HOUSE

Capricorns are good, stable partners. They tend to take relationships seriously because they take most things seriously. If you're looking for some rowdy spontaneity, this may not be your sign. But if you're looking for a responsible and steady partner, Capricorn is a perfect fit. They do make work a priority, though, so be aware of that. The typical Capricorn is ambitious, so be ready to support them in their career pursuits. This could mean they have less time to spend at home. As far as communication goes, Capricorns speak from a place of logic. They do have a propensity to complain, but if you give them a shoulder to lean on, they'll move on pretty quickly. They don't like to ruminate on negative emotions. Sometimes Capricorn needs someone to lift them up and show them how to embrace silliness. If you're up for the challenge, you'll have a steady partner for life.

Tenth house people often value careers even more than Capricorns. If your partner is a 10th house Sun, they need you to support them in their career aspirations and endeavors. This may mean that you need to stay home with the kids, while they act as the main breadwinner. For 10th house individuals, it's not just about a paycheck. They need a true vocation--a job that makes them feel like they are using their uniqueness for the greater good. They like to act as an authority of some sort in their careers. So don't try to get them to cut back on their hours or pursue something that doesn't align with their core identities. These people can be stubborn in that regard, but they're also impressive and determined individuals.

SUN IN AQUARIUS OR SUN IN THE 11TH HOUSE

Aquarius is detached and cerebral, but a pleasant conversationalist nonetheless. They may shy away from conflict or certain emotional topics, but they tend to be deep and hate superficiality. If you want to have intellectual conversations about life and society, date an Aquarius. Aquarians can sometimes be a tad socially awkward. They tend to be introverted, so you may need to work to bring them out of their shell. But you can always count on them to try and maintain peace and calm. Aquarians need direct communicators in their lives, because they find it hard to be direct themselves, so be patient with them and enjoy the tender, gentle presence they bring.

Eleventh house people are similar to 10th house people in that their contribution to society is of paramount importance. Friendships are also important with this placement. These are the people who like to be involved in multiple clubs and communities and want to offer something unique to each one. They're deeply concerned with the outside world, so they need plenty of space to go out, get involved, and make a difference to humanity. If your friendships are important to you too, you may prove a great match for an 11th house Sun. They often find their soulmates through their friendships or communities. Eleventh house people also have big dreams, so it's important not to stifle that. They're capable of achieving great things, so let them go after what they want in life.

SUN IN PISCES OR SUN IN THE 12TH HOUSE

Pisces, like Leo, loves to be in love, but for different reasons. Pisces crave romantic emotional connection-- it's their favorite thing in the world. But since Pisces is so nebulous and sponge-like, it tends toward one of two extremes: an all-encompassing spiritual kind of love, or a pulling away. Sometimes, Pisces are so overwhelmed by the emotions of others that they pull away.

But with some direct communication, you can bring them back into the fold. You must be willing to enter their emotional world with them and be prepared for a fair number of tantrums. Much like Aries, Pisces lack a filter, but with Pisces it's more of an emotional filter. But it's nice to always know where you stand with them. They're not ones to let emotions simmer below the surface. If you enjoy direct emotional communication, Pisces is the sign for you. To win them over, try communicating with them through abstract means, such as art, music, or poetry.

The 12th house is hard to describe in a simple, succinct way. It's the house of the subconscious and the imagination. But it's also considered to be the house where the planets go to get lost. Often, when planets are in the 12th house, their true expression is suppressed into the subconscious. This can breed a great deal of insecurity if the individual lacks awareness. At the same time, though, 12th house Suns are very in tune with others and with humanity in general. They can feel things that others cannot, and they're often very empathetic when they have the strength to own their empathy. Mood swings may be inevitable. But your 12th house partner will constantly inspire you with their mystical and poetic view of the world. They usually have a caring disposition and much artistic talent.

When it comes to using astrology as a tool, the more information the better. Before looking into things like Mercury placements and synastry charts, focus on individual birth charts. Get a sense of the overall energy, then hone in on the more specific placements and chart connections. It can feel complex and daunting, but astrology requires that you build an overall picture of things. Each part of a horoscope affects the rest, so you need a fully-synthesized perspective in order to accurately interpret everything. But once you're well-versed in chart analysis, things like synastry and composite charts will blow your mind. You can get incredibly specific and detailed with your interpretations as well. Consider purchasing a synastry chart reading so you can develop a better understand of what I've been talking about. You'll likely be quite impressed.

ASTROLOGY AND SUCCESS

Astrology can be an incredible tool for unearthing what you want out of life, how to optimize your potential, and what success means to you. There's much to consider when it comes to success…things like work ethic, passions, natural talents and your relationship to achievement and finances. All of these topics are accounted for in a birth chart, you simply have to know what to look for. Additionally, astrology can act as a sort of map or cheat sheet.

MOON PHASES

You don't have to be a master of transits in order to learn how to time things to work out in your favor.

This can be an especially useful skill in business, or merely for deciding the best time to apply for jobs. For example, it's very easy to track the moon. You can always discover the next moon phase through a Google search, but I'll break it down for you anyway.

New Moon

New Moons occur once a month and, unsurprisingly, they mark an excellent time for new beginnings. If you want to initiate a new project or start the ball rolling on an idea, a new moon-day is a great day to do it. If you want, you can get more in-depth, and find out which sign contains the new moon, and that sign will slightly alter the tone of the new moon. If it's a new moon in Pisces, for example, it could be a good time to start a creative project. But if it's a new moon in Capricorn, you may want to set a business motion in plan. Sometimes, though, New Moons simply bring fresh ideas. If you try to accomplish too much during the New Moon, you might find holes in your ideas later on, which means you'll have to start over again. This is the time to listen to your gut and make plans accordingly.

First Quarter Moon

By the First Quarter Moon, you have put your plans in motion, and now it's time to make important decisions about those plans. Once you've started something, you have to ask yourself more questions. You have to figure out the details, and you have to be prepared for whatever obstacles arise throughout the creation process. This is the time to get your hands dirty and test your ability to handle crises and setbacks. The moon appears to be about 50 percent lit during a First Quarter Moon, so it's important to foster the growth of your project and take action. This is the hard work phase, when you'll use a great deal of energy to see your vision through. With the moon as your support, you can get through it with confidence and ease.

Full Moon

Full Moons also occur once a month, but the energy they bring differs from that of a New Moon. Full Moons represent completion, so they offer an opportunity to tie up loose ends and finish things before you move forward. A full moon can also signify some kind of resolution to whatever you started during the New Moon. Ideally, you should work to make this time your final deadline; the point where you aim to have your project fully completed because the energy at this time is ripe for completion. It's also a great time for editing. The moon is fully lit, so that final detail that you need may arrive like a lightning bolt in your mind. This time marks the ending of something.

Third Quarter Moon

The Third Quarter Moon piggy-backs off of the Waning Gibbous Moon. It's a time to make decisions about your process, such as what needs to change and what could use improvement. These are the questions you should be asking yourself. Most likely, you will have to make some important decisions during this period of the month. Once you start keeping track of the moon, you'll be shocked to see how often life events naturally occur according to the moon's rhythms.

Finally, when it comes to the moon, be sure to check its placement in regard to your own sun sign placement. When the moon is in the same sign as your sun, you can make positive advancements. But if it's opposite your sun, you may want to lay low for the time being.

THE MIDHEAVEN

If you're new to astrology, you have probably never heard of the midheaven, which is also known as the MC. You can find the MC at the top center of every chart. Whatever sign contains your MC shows how you are meant to publicly present yourself. It can also reveal something about the type of career you are drawn to/meant to engage in. If you have a Gemini midheaven, for example, you may be drawn to a career that involves travel or communication. If you have a Scorpio midheaven, you may crave a position of power, or you might want to delve beneath the surface of things by becoming a psychotherapist.

The midheaven also shows how you appear to the public. If you're an Aries Sun but you have Cancer at the midheaven, you may appear to the public sweeter and more feminine than the way you really feel. Understanding this can help you decide what career path you want to take, and it can also shed light on how others see you.

THE PLANETS

The other planets can also indicate a great deal about career and financial timing. Some planets, in particular, are career or money planets. Venus, for example, is often associated with financial gain or loss because it represents values and rules Taurus. When Venus is retrograding, it can bring a time in which your financial situation is uncertain or is going through some sort of transition. But then when it goes direct, it could bring a promotion, or money could come to you seemingly out of nowhere. Jupiter is also a planet associated with financial gains and losses, so you can track Jupiter's movement the same way. If Jupiter is about to hit your natal Venus, for instance, this is a very lucky financial time. Unless, of course, you've been spending frivolously left and right. Then, Jupiter might try to teach you a lesson. Saturn can have a similar effect. If Saturn hits your natal Venus, it could be a time when you need to budget, but after it passes, you'll have new discipline when it comes to spending and earning money.

Outside of transits, how can you use astrology to assist you in your career pursuits, especially if you haven't landed on your dream career yet? Well, if you know your three main signs, you're already on your way to understanding what kind of careers might interest you. Each personality type has strengths and weaknesses that bode better for some careers over others. Start by reflecting on your signs and general temperament, and ask yourself if the things you're pursuing challenge your development as much as you'd like them to.

Saturn

Saturn is essentially the career and success planet. Since it rules Capricorn, the *sign* of career and success, its placement can reveal a lot about what careers you might be drawn to. It also reveals a lot about how you approach a career and success. Saturn can feel restrictive in the first couple of decades of life, but it blossoms after the Saturn Return at twenty-eight-years-old.

If you have Saturn in Capricorn, you may resent authority and hate the idea of being responsible until you hit 30, at which point you may actually crave a leadership position with a lot of responsibility. If you have Saturn in Aquarius, you may pursue a comfortable position where you can blend in with the crowd, or be on your own. But after your Saturn Return, you may want to provide something more unique to your community. You may feel challenged to lend your unique skills in a more public or creative way. Look at which house Saturn is placed in as well. If it's in your 7th house, for example, part of your journey to success might have to do with building important relationships. If it falls in your 12th house, you may be inclined to help others or to use your imagination in some way.

The 2nd House & Taurus

The 2nd house indicates what you find most valuable in life. It's also the house of money, security, and self-esteem. So it's obviously helpful to look at your 2nd house to decide what might interest you with regard to your career and your lifestyle. Depending on what signs and planets are placed there, you might value a life of financial wealth, or you may prefer a more minimalistic life.

If you have Sagittarius in the 2nd, you'll want a lot of whatever you value. Often this placement brings financial luck, but also the capacity for overspending. If you have Taurus there, you'll prefer to work slowly toward the life you want, with caution and care. All of the Earth signs and houses offer illuminating information on the subject of career and success. Go ahead and look at where Taurus is placed in your chart as well. This will further highlight your unique values.

The 6th House & Virgo

If you're curious about your work ethic and your general approach toward work, you need to look to the 6th house. The 6th house rules Virgo, so it's all about daily routines, rituals, and practical maintenance. Obviously, it's important to consider your work approach when thinking about career and success. If you crave a lot of freedom in your daily routine, you might not pursue a life as a doctor, for instance. If you have Aquarius in your 6th, it's a fair assumption that you'll need a lot of freedom and variety in your daily life. It also suggests that you'll need a work environment that is ethical and humanitarian.

If you have Leo in your 6th, you'll want to shine through your work and you'll need an outlet to express your individuality. Planets that fall in the 6th also shed light on how you approach work. If you have Saturn there, you may have trouble disciplining yourself. Or you might overcompensate, and be exceptionally self-disciplined. If you have Uranus there, you'll probably want to approach work in an unorthodox way, like while watching television or talking to friends. Look to where Virgo is in your chart to gain some deeper insight.

The 10th House & Capricorn

The 10th house is similar to the midheaven since the 10th house is always at the top center of the birth chart. More often than not, the sign that contains the midheaven will also be the ruler of your 10th house. But sometimes this isn't the case. It all depends on where your 10th starts and ends. For example, half of your 10th house might have Gemini, while the other half occupies Cancer. The midheaven might be in Cancer but your 10th house is still ruled by Gemini. If so, both Gemini and Cancer will color the way you approach career and success.

The 10th house is the house of career. It shows how you feel about success, ambition, and your public reputation. Whether or not you know what sign rules your 10th house, you're probably already aware of your passions and ambitions. So look at your chart and see how accurate it is. See if it helps you to perceive your ambitions in a new way.

Mars

Mars is also a good planet to consider when thinking about career and success. Since it shows how you use your drive, and how you go about getting what you want, it's especially relevant here. Plus, Mars indicates how you use your energy, and you need a lot of energy to build a career or get ahead in life. If you have Mars in Aries, you may pursue a sport or something that allows you to feel larger than life. If you have Mars in Virgo, you may want to be a massage therapist or something else that deals with health and body issues.

The house that contains Mars also sheds light on this. If you have Mars in the 5th house, creativity and self-expression should be important to you. If you have it in the 11th, you'll want to give something to your community. Exploring your Mars sign and house can also help you when it comes to understanding your work ethic. Do you go after what you want with full force? Without doubting yourself? Or do you do it more tentatively? Maybe you go after things in a covert way. Look to your Mars placement to find out.

Sun & Moon

It may seem obvious but the Sun/Moon signs, and their house placements, are also important to consider when thinking about career. Since the sun sign shows what qualities you are meant to harness for ego development, it would be wise to pursue a career that challenges the qualities of your sun sign.

The sun shows where you naturally want to shine in life, so if your job supports that want, it's a win-win. It tends to happen quite naturally since the sun sign is such an important part of our overall personalities. While all the different "career points" are necessary to consider, the sun sign is equally important. Likewise, the moon sign is a substantial component of our personalities, so many gravitate toward careers that utilize the moon, especially if the moon has more emphasis in the natal chart.

ASTROLOGY AND CAREERS

With all this in mind, let's explore the different ways each of the signs view careers and what qualities these people should look for in their vocations.

Aries Careers

Aries needs to do something that requires a great deal of energy and passion. The most common careers connected to Aries are in athletics and the military. Aries individuals have a secret longing to feel heroic, so anything that embraces heroism is ideal. They also excel at fighting for others, so many Aries are drawn to fields in politics or social work, where they can advocate for others. They also make great salespeople because they're determined and competitive. No matter what they pursue, it has to be something that allows them to express their passions and raw fighting power. Ideally, their career should allow them to feel larger than life, even if that means being a big fish in a small pond.

Taurus Careers

Taurus has a finely-tuned relationship with aestheticism, so capitalizing on that is always ideal when pursuing a career. Things such as design, art, cooking and flipping houses would make good options for any Taurus. Ultimately, though, Taurus has to lean on its core values when considering a career.

Taureans can become easily depressed if they're stuck in a job that does nothing beyond providing them with financial security. But since financial security is so important to these people, they can easily fall into that trap. If you're a Taurus, make sure your job is valuable in more ways than just fiscally. Many Taureans also make great politicians or critics because they have strong opinions and they're so good at understanding form.

Gemini Careers

Geminis are great at careers involving communication or that let them often experience new things. They make great Project Managers, as long the job primarily involves helping different parties communicate with each other. They're also excellent at Public Relations, or any job that lets them be the voice of an organization, such as radio announcer or television news broadcaster. Geminis won't do well with any job that requires them to perform routine tasks over and over.

Cancer Careers

Cancers are natural caretakers so they may pursue jobs that allow them to nurture in some way. Careers like veterinarians, doctors, gardeners, and teachers are all ideal. The water signs have another secret skill though - they're very good at selling things to people. The best salespeople are able to intuit how others feel, so it's no wonder Cancer has a talent for this. Additionally, people don't give Cancers enough credit for their creative abilities.

Many astrologers think that Cancers are even more creative than Leos. The water signs also have a gift for turning their emotions into humor. So any of these outlets are great for the sensitive Cancer. The worst job for Cancer is usually one where they can't be social or feel needed by others.

Leo Careers

The obvious choice for Leo careers is in the realm of performance, where they can shine in the spotlight. But there are a variety of careers that Leo excels at. Many make gifted therapists because they're so interested in understanding themselves and others. They make great teachers, because they have an inspirational quality and they feed off the energy of young people.

Anything creative is ideal because Leo needs to express itself as a unique individual. A job that is inherently fun or exciting, like a club promoter or DJ, is also appealing. Leos are often great public speakers and leaders. Barack Obama is a Leo.

Virgo Careers

Virgos tend to be extremely critical, so they should pursue careers that allow them to use their critical skills. They also need to serve others in some way. Virgo has a very helpful quality to it, so functions best when it can be of service to someone or some cause. This means there are a wide variety of career possibilities for Virgo. They excel in the technology field because they care about details.

They also make great music producers, architects, and editors. I've already shared their relationship to sex and the body, so there are plenty of careers in those areas that would be suitable for Virgos. And, of course, they thrive in the role of critic. This is why they can also make great teachers, professors, and mentors.

Libra Careers

Libras tend to be lazy, so they need a career that allows them to procrastinate or have a good deal of freedom. They loathe injustice of any kind, so they make good lawyers or activists. And since they have such a strong relationship with the concept of beauty, they make excellent designers and artists.

Debate is another avenue they may pursue because they have strong opinions and know how to play devil's advocate. In addition, more than any other sign, Libras tend to love animals, so working with animals in some capacity may be ideal. They also make great physical trainers because they know how to look good, so naturally they can help others look good as well.

Scorpio Careers

Scorpio should pursue careers that allow them to embrace the dark and mysterious. Things like psychotherapy, life insurance, criminal investigation and funeral worker could prove fulfilling. Many pursue a life as a doctor, because they're so accepting of death, and their sensitive nature makes them feel good when they're needed. Anything that allows them to get down and dirty with life's darkness is appropriate.

Scorpio is the most emotionally strong sign of the zodiac, so they can handle it all. They also make great philosophers and writers. Many are also great actors because they can so effortlessly tune into others' emotions. Music, and especially songwriting, could prove attractive as well, as could poetry.

Sagittarius Careers

Sagittarians are meant to inspire and uplift others with their expansive perspective on life. They need to pursue a career with lots of room for growth, where they can constantly develop themselves and learn more and more about the world. They also need a healthy amount of freedom and variety, so any career that involves travel is ideal. Since Sagittarius has such a knack for language, they make great translators or reporters. They can also make entertaining talk-show hosts. They're quick-witted and vivacious, so anything that allows them to put their personalities on display is usually quite fulfilling. Additionally, Sagittarius is always looking for deeper meaning, so they make excellent writers and philosophers.

Capricorn Careers

As an earth sign, Capricorns do well with careers that require organization and patience, and often tend to be attracted to careers that become highly important to them. Whether it's being a teacher in a class full of unruly students or an accountant at tax time, Capricorns are able to buckle-down and get things done where others might throw in the towel.

Aquarius Careers

Aquarians need to do something creative with their lives, whether big or small. Their minds are always coming up with new ideas, so the most common Aquarius career is an inventor, but they also make great artists and humanitarians. Like Virgo, Aquarius needs to help people in order to feel satisfied, a trait which harkens back to the myth of Prometheus.

Good careers for Aquarians include therapists, activists, political leaders, writers, and entrepreneurs. It's also important that they have a job that allows them to use their intellect in some way. They need to be intellectually challenged and stimulated or they'll be bored. But if they can help people while also using their mind, they've got a fulfilling career.

Pisces Careers

Pisces is another sign that should pursue something creative. Oftentimes, Pisces are too messy to pursue something rigid and corporate. However, they also make good salespeople because they can enter the minds of others. Music and acting are popular choices for this reason. Many Pisces also make excellent teachers and therapists because these jobs allow them to utilize their sensitivity and ability to connect with others.

Other artistic avenues are also desirable, such as writing and painting. Pisces, maybe more than any other sign, can easily become depressed in a lifeless nine-to-five job. They need to pursue something that makes them feel connected to the rest of life. Otherwise, they'll drink too much and take out their frustrations on others.

There are plenty of career horoscopes you can seek out for a more complete interpretation. But by analyzing each of these chart points, you can learn a great deal about what kind of career would best suit you. It's important to keep an open mind. Often when it comes to a career, part of us wants one thing, while another part wants something entirely different. Astrology can help us identify what these different parts want, and how to arrive at a compromise between them. And even if you already have an established career, analyzing your chart this way can help you discover if you're in need of a hobby or other external outlet.

FINAL WORDS

By this point, hopefully you've gathered that astrology is a massive and complex system. It goes much deeper than sun sign horoscopes. The truth is, as soon as you think you know all there is to know, there's even more to learn. If you've made it to this point in the book, you know astrology harkens back to ancient Babylonia and has strong ties to ancient Greek mythology. Throughout history it's been used as a tool for geniuses and common folk alike. It can be used for personality assessment, prediction, and gaining a better understanding of the people in your daily life. Some even use it for match-making. It's used it as a supplement to psychology, and as a means to obtain a sense of ancestry and psychological inheritance. The number of ways you can use astrology in your everyday life never ceases to amaze me. If everyone knew the basics and embraced it for the helpful lens that it is, I think there would be a richer appreciation of humanity and a deeper understanding of our purpose here on Earth.

This book is a stepping stone for those who know little about astrology but want to gain a deeper understanding. In order to see how fascinating it is, to feel like one of the ancients studying the moon to reap better crops, you have to carry it with you throughout your daily life. This means knowing the signs of the people around you. Until you start looking for astrological consistencies in your daily life, you'll only have a superficial experience. It's easy to be skeptical because it's the kind of experience you can't simply read about; you have to live it to understand its accuracy. But that means you have to have a more complex understanding of it than the horoscope writers at BuzzFeed. If it seems too overwhelming, start with the elements: Fire, Earth, Air, and Water. Many people exude one of these temperaments... if you have a friend with a fiery personality, ask them if they're an Aries. Look up the signs of some of your favorite celebrities. Ideally, if you are able to get the birth times of the people close to you, you can expedite the process and apply everything in this book toward understanding those individuals. But if that's impossible, just start with the basics.

Once you have a more nuanced and experiential feel for each of the signs, you won't be able to stop seeing astrology in everything you do and see. Listening to others go on about sun signs may have seemed a bit annoying in the past, but there's a reason those who have embraced astrology love to talk about it so much. It makes you feel powerful. Suddenly, you see the world around you through a more complex, outside perspective. Everything has new meaning in a new context. You'll understand how to appeal to people depending on their unique personality. You'll also have new confidence when it comes to initiating projects and planning for the future. You have a higher understanding of things that you can manipulate in your favor. It's like when people feel more powerful after learning psychology; it gives you a leg up. So don't criticize your girlfriend for putting too much weight on the stars and symbols. Chances are, they know you better than you know yourself. Luckily, though, now you too have access to this brilliant ancient wisdom.

www.ingramcontent.com/pod-product-compliance
Lightning Source LLC
Chambersburg PA
CBHW071453070526
44578CB00001B/330